HE[NRI]

IN M[Y] OWN [WORDS]

Edited and Compiled by
Robert Durback

DARTON · LONGMAN + TODD

First published in Great Britain in 2002 by
Darton, Longman and Todd Ltd
1 Spencer Court
140–142 Wandsworth High Street
London SW18 4JJ

Reprinted 2002

First published in the USA in 2001 by
Liguori Publications, Liguori, Missouri

ISBN 0–232–52463–7

A catalogue record for this book is available from the British Library.

Printed and bound in Great Britain by
Page Bros, Norwich, Norfolk

CONTENTS

FOREWORD

One evening after Henri had celebrated the Eucharist in our small chapel in Daybreak, Michael made it clear to his assistant that he wanted to "get to" Henri. He had something to say. Michael is an extrovert, loves people, and loves to talk! He is also a man with a disability, radically slowed down as a result of medication.

Henri was deep in conversation with someone else and there were a few people waiting to speak to him, but Michael was not discouraged. They waited. Finally Henri turned to Michael who began with, "I…I….I wwwant to say something."

Henri bent down to listen and said, "OK Michael, what is it?"

Michael pulled himself up and began, "I…I…I wwwant to ttttell you that you tttttalked good tonight." Michael was referring to Henri's homily on the Eucharist about bread that was broken to be given, just as our lives are broken to be given. The topic was intellectually challenging for Michael, but he had obviously heard something in Henri's words.

Michael said again, pointing with his finger at his heart, Yyyyyou…yyyyyou…yyyou talked so good tonight! I llllistened to you and your wwwwords went right in here. Yyyyour wwwords went rrrrright in here…iiin my heart!"

Henri suddenly straightened up and with a look of great tenderness and sincerity said, "Thank you Michael.

What an incredible man you are. When you listen, you hear goodness!"

Was Henri just being kind? Michael could not possibly have understood the homily. But Michael really heard something that touched his heart because his heart is attuned to hear the Word, to hear goodness. And in the spiritual journey when the heart is attuned, the Word often bypasses the mind and penetrates the spirit. Henri, in his homily, spoke authentically, and Michael listened with the ears of his open heart. The Word, like an arrow, pierced, touched, and inspired Michael—in his heart.

I believe that Henri would have liked nothing better than to write a book entitled, *Henri Nouwen: In My Own Words*! He just never thought about it! "In My Own Words" summarizes his life as teacher, lecturer, pastor, and writer. Henri's books are well known not because they are well researched, scholarly, or erudite. They are appreciated because they speak his life journey and the insights that touched his heart, "in his own words." Based on his knowledge of the Gospel, on listening to others, and on his personal experience of suffering, friendship, hope, joy, anguish, or peace, he spoke and he wrote, "in his own words." So, a whole book of "In My Own Words" would, I believe, have given him great pleasure!

Who better to do such a book in Henri's name than his friend of twenty-five years, Bob Durback. Bob was Henri's good, faithful, interested, enthusiastic, friend. He and Henri loved to get together for spirited conversations about everything but mostly about the things Henri was saying in his published articles and books. Bob took

Henri's every word seriously, and Henri loved nothing better than to meet with Bob when he was questioning something, spoken or written. Talk about animated! They were diving for the words to put meaning on the concepts. It was stimulating to observe them in conversation and to be party to their wonderful questions and insights. They deeply engaged each other!

Bob is, I believe, the greatest living reference of Henri's works. Henri knew it and he said it many times before he died. Since then I don't know how many times I have called or advised others to call Bob to ask where Henri said or wrote this or that! He laughs but he knows the answer. And when he calls me with a question my first reaction is panic as I think, "What is he going to ask and will I know what he is talking about? What will he think of me if I don't know the answer?" But Bob is like Henri. He only wants to deepen and to grow in authenticity. He is not looking to "catch" anyone. His whole life is about friendship, finding God, loving, and deepening. Bob is not only our best reference person but he is an amazing friend.

Henri Nouwen: In My Own Words is Henri at his best! Bob sets the direction and then gives Henri the stage to inspire us with his life and his wisdom. Occasionally there is a small commentary by the editor to ensure that we are not just letting Henri perform, but that we are engaged, listening personally, identifying with, and taking to heart the wisdom of the one who walked before us. Bob insists that the book is not just about Henri but also about you and I on our journey through transformation.

Readers, let Michael inspire and guide you in your reading of this book. He brings an open heart, ready to hear beyond the words and ready to be pierced by the truth!" Do the same for your own inspiration and nourishment because Henri "talks good" in this book. I hope that "when you listen, you [also] hear goodness."

SUE MOSTELLER, C.S.J.
HENRI NOUWEN LITERARY CENTRE
TORONTO, CANADA
MARCH 2001

$\mathcal{A}$CKNOWLEDGMENTS

I welcome the opportunity to say "thank you" to the many friends without whom I could never have completed the task of letting Henri Nouwen speak to readers, both new and old, in his own words. My first word of thanks must go to Sue Mosteller of the Henri Nouwen Literary Center, who not only gave her warm and loving support by word but also filled my arms with documentation most helpful to me in my work. I am grateful to her assistants, Maureen Wright and Mary Lou Daquano and the entire L'Arche Community of Daybreak who form the link that keeps me intimately connected with the mentor and guide who has made such a difference in my life.

I offer a special word of gratitude to Jeanne Koma who gave timely help in reading and making valuable suggestions for improving the text. And my warmest thanks to Patricia Kelly and the Carmelite Sisters in Reno, to Mary Ann Flannery and the Vincentian Sisters of Charity, and to Mary Lavin and the Carmelite Sisters in Cleveland, for their faithful prayer support throughout my work on the book. As always, a special word of thanks to Francis Kline and my brothers at Mepkin Abbey in South Carolina who these many years have been for me a home away from home.

I wish to thank Patricia Kossmann, who encouraged me in my writing and was the first to approach me on behalf of Liguori Publications. And Judy Bauer who has shown such patience and gentle humor in waiting through the many delays and movable deadline dates.

I reserve for Ruthanne Fait a most profound bow for her exceptional generosity in volunteering to bear the workload involved in a book of this nature, including the sweat work of transferring previously published material onto disks and into printouts for my editorial scrutiny and recycling. Most of all, I want to thank her for the friendship that has grown out of this collaborative effort. I welcome the opportunity to acknowledge my debt to the community of St. Peter Parish that has been such an abundant source of inspiration and so many blessings for me under the leadership of its pastor, Father Robert Marrone.

I save for dessert: My special gratitude to John Eudes Bamberger and the monks of Genesee Abbey, without whom it could never have happened!

JANUARY 24, 2001
SIXTY-NINTH ANNIVERSARY OF
THE BIRTH OF HENRI J. M. NOUWEN

$\mathcal{I}$NTRODUCTION

I remember very clearly the moment of my first meeting with Henri Nouwen. In September 1974, I had driven from Cleveland to the Abbey of the Genesee, a Trappist monastery in Upstate New York, for a weekend retreat. Slipping into the chapel, I took my place among the guests, chanting Vesper psalms along with the monks. As we chanted, a single face among the monks caught my attention. I had seen that face before. But where? I could not make the connection.

After the Mass following Vespers, I made my way to the lobby, where books were on display for sale. One of them caught my eye. "Oh look!" I pointed out to one of the guests whom I had befriended, "There's a new book by Henri Nouwen!" "He's here, you know," she offered without hesitation. And at that moment I was enlightened about the strange face I had recognized among the monks, but could not identify. It was the face of Henri Nouwen. "What was he doing here?" I wondered. The guest, a nun from the area, obligingly unraveled the mystery: Nouwen was on sabbatical from Yale and was living in community with the monks for a period of seven months. Now I understood why I had difficulty recognizing his face: His head was shaved!

There, in the back seat of my car, I mused, was my collection of newspapers and magazines carrying his recently published articles. And here he was, living with the monks in this monastery. From that moment on, I was carried on a wave of expectation: the possibility of a personal encounter with one I had come to admire as a guide for my own spiritual journey.

Finally, I went to see the abbot, John Eudes Bamberger. We had been in the novitiate together at Gethsemani Abbey in 1950 and had remained connected over the years. It was our friendship that brought me periodically to Genesee. As we sat and chatted in the abbot's office, I mentioned how surprised—and delighted—I was to find Henri Nouwen living in the midst of the community. I did not ask to have any meeting arranged. I asked only one simple concession: If I should happen to cross paths with Nouwen while walking the monastery grounds, could I speak to him? Permission granted. All I needed now was to be lucky enough to meet Nouwen while walking the road from the retreat house to the abbey church. A slim possibility.

I had arrived at the abbey late Friday afternoon. I would be leaving Monday after a quick lunch in the guest kitchen. Monday came all too soon. My chances of meeting Henri Nouwen had run out. It was time to head back to Cleveland. After throwing all my bags into my car, I popped into the abbot's office for a last farewell. I said my good-bye, received the abbot's blessing, and headed for my car, parked just outside. The hall space between the abbot's door and the door to the outside was only two or three steps. As I was walking those steps a door opened farther down the hall to my left. Through that door walked Henri Nouwen. For me, this was an Easter moment.

As Nouwen approached I smiled and said, "You don't

know me, but I know you!" He returned the smile, offering his handshake, and began speaking animatedly, asking me all sorts of questions about myself, all this time following me to my car as we continued the lively conversation. I was in no hurry to climb into my car, and he obviously was in no hurry to bring an end to the conversation. He was interested in the fact that I had been a novice at Gethsemani along with John Eudes, during the years Merton was publishing his books. He was also interested in the fact that I had spent an additional nine years at Mepkin Abbey, another foundation of Gethsemani, in South Carolina.

Of particular interest to him was the information I passed on regarding the Merton tapes, tapes of talks Merton gave regularly to his novices at Gethsemani, only recently released and available to the public for the first time from a small outlet in New York. He responded with enthusiasm: "I would like to get a set for the library at Yale Divinity School." I promised I would send him an order form as soon as I got home. He pressed further: "Could you come back for another visit next month?" I told him I regretted I could not, but would certainly keep in touch by mail.

The limits on my time with Henri Nouwen at this first meeting turned out to be a blessing. When you can't visit with a friend face to face, you write letters. In this case, my new friend turned out to be a prolific writer. The meeting opened the door to a correspondence that would last until Nouwen's death some twenty-two years later. I received my first handwritten letter from Nouwen three weeks later, dated September 23, 1974.

This meeting at the abbey would be the first of three over a three-year period. In all three instances, the meetings were coincidental, not planned. Each of us had followed our own travel schedules independently of the other. In the third instance, I did indeed attempt, in collusion with the abbot, to time a visit that would coincide with a visit by Nouwen, I had to give up. Nouwen had planned visits and twice had to cancel.

Finally, I wrote to the abbot and told him I could wait no longer; that I would drive to the abbey on November 1 to celebrate All Saints' Day before the snows of winter set in. Agreed. I pulled into the parking lot outside the church just in time for Night Prayer. Darkness had already fallen. I hurried into the church to find the first empty stall. And who was standing right there in the stall next to me, but Henri Nouwen.

It was during this visit that I asked Henri if I could drive him to the airport for his return trip. He accepted, and I welcomed the opportunity for the extended visit. We continued the discussion at the airport with the little time we had left. When it was time to board, we shook hands and said "Good-bye." But as Nouwen began his walk to the gate he suddenly wheeled around and said: "Would you like to come and spend a week with me at Yale?" Less than four months later I was packing my bags for Yale. It was February 1977. It became a yearly event until Nouwen submitted his resignation and left Yale to test his calling to work as a missionary in Latin America in October 1981. (See *Gracias! A Latin America Journal*.)

We stayed in touch by mail, telephone, and

subsequent visits over the ensuing years. My favorite story from this period is the letter I received from Nouwen that read: "Bob, I just got a letter from *Reader's Digest*. They want to publish a quote of mine they found in Forbes magazine, and they want to know which of my books it comes from. Can you find it for me?" I walked over to my bookcase, pulled *Out of Solitude* off the shelf, opened it up to a place I had underlined, and sure enough, there was the quote. From then on Henri enjoyed using the incident as a party joke, telling his friends in so many words, that if he ever needed to find out where he had said something, all he would have to do was push my button, and out it would come, complete with page number and paragraph.

From this context emerged years later, a theme book, culled from Nouwen's writings, which eventually became *Seeds of Hope: A Henri Nouwen Reader*.

When Judy Bauer of Liguori Publications asked more recently if I would gather a new collection of quotes from the writings of Henri Nouwen, I willingly agreed and took delight in revisiting familiar territory. As my collection grew and it came time to make decisions with regard to how I would bring the many diverse strands of thought into a unity, my first priority was simplicity. I made a special point of keeping the table of contents to six basic ideas: They suggested themselves to me in this order: *setting; awareness; response; turning point; commitment; completion*.

Why these six and no others? *Setting* by its very nature gives us a starting point. All stories begin with: "Once upon a time...." The *setting* is the stage, the backdrop, the initial point of reference from which the whole play unfolds. We will come back to the setting after we review what the rest of the story is about. The story is about you, the reader. You will be invited to identify with the author, Henri Nouwen, as he tells his story. *Awareness, response, turning point, commitment,* and *completion* are five ways of being alive. I see in them the five dynamics that power a human life to move from stagnancy to growth and fulfillment. When one of them is missing, something may be missing from your life. The gift of *awareness* in particular has fallen upon hard times these days. The advances of modern technology and growth of the media and advertising industries have made it possible to be entertained, informed and distracted twenty-four hours a day, seven days a week. Never has it been so easy to escape from our inner selves, from that scourge we all dread: loneliness. Never has it been more important to reclaim in our lives the gift of awareness.

Awareness is not so much about analyzing or figuring out as it is about just being alive to the gift of the present moment. Or the gift of a special person. Moments of awareness are not always pleasant moments. One may be left with the awareness of one's loneliness: the death of a loved one, the loss of a job, the end of a marriage. Part II—after an appropriate setting of the stage in Part I— will deal with the dimensions of *Awareness* with particular attention to self-awareness, awareness of the world around us, and, if we are to be fully in touch with reality, awareness of God.

Part III is summed up in the word *Response*. Once we become aware of the world around us—or within us—we inevitably *respond* in some way. We accept or reject. We celebrate or mourn. We take action or we choose to ignore. What we cannot escape is the decision to respond. As you view Nouwen's responses to what he perceives within and outside of himself, compare. How does the memory of your responses to life compare with his?

Part IV brings us to *Turning Point*, to the crises in our lives, and to the centerpiece of the book, Nouwen's account of the story of *The Return of the Prodigal Son* as portrayed in Rembrandt's painting by the same name. Here, especially, the reader is invited to ask: Where do I fit into this picture? With which one of the characters in the story can I identify? Is there a single period in my life in which I could say I lived out—or am living out—a part of this story?

Part V brings us to another climactic point summed up in the word *Commitment*. We often speak loosely of commitments. We are committed to our families. We are committed to our own personal values, we are committed to our local communities, to social justice, to our long-term plans for the future. Sometimes we are just committed for the evening or the weekend. Part V deals with commitment painted large. What am I going to do with the rest of my life? Is there any room in my life for God? How do I integrate into my busy day my spiritual values and my relationship with God?

Part VI brings us to *Completion*: not only to the end of the book, but to the end of our lives. Recently a homilist pointed out the difference in the way movies in our country ended years ago: When the movie was over viewers would see on the screen in big letters the words: "The End." Today, he pointed out, movies end instead with the major character or characters riding off into the sunset, and we know it's the end without having to be told.

The homilist then went on to point out how European movies announced the end, not with the words "The End," but with "*Finis*," which carries a different shade of meaning, namely, the notion of completeness: "It is complete." It is with this idea in mind that I have chosen the word *completion* to end the book with Nouwen's thoughts on death and dying. Nouwen sees death not as the dreaded, unavoidable catastrophe that brings an end to our lives, but as the grand climax that brings our lives to completion.

It is time now to dim the lights and focus attention on center stage, where we await the appearance of our storyteller. I draw this image of stage and setting not from sheer fantasy, but from one of my early experiences of visiting with Henri Nouwen at Yale. I was walking through one of the halls and noticed a sign posted on a bulletin board: "Henri Nouwen to give presentation on van Gogh," with all the details of time and place. Luckily for me, the show was scheduled for one of the evenings during the week of my visit. This was to be no boring lecture. It would be my first look at Henri the writer turned Henri the showman, complete with stage props.

First of all, he had two people planted in the audience:

one a piano player, the other to run a slide projector. All either needed was a glance from Henri to know what to do and when to do it. Henri himself used the simplest of stage props to achieve maximum effect. He brought in an ordinary household lamp with shade, set it on top of a post, positioned himself next to it, with a small cap on his head and a shawl wrapped around his neck and draped over his shoulder. The effect was clear and needed no explanation: It was late at night. He was standing under a streetlight and inviting us to listen as he reminisced about his brother, Vincent. Henri was no longer Henri. He was Theo, Vincent van Gogh's brother, and he was going to tell us all about his brother, the artist. With perfect timing and eye signals picked up by the piano player and the slide projectionist, the show went on without a glitch. We saw lavish splashes of golden sunlight; shimmering fields of ocher, emerald, scarlet, and ermine; blossoming fruit trees and tulips, poppies and sunflowers. And yes, the hard life of "The Potato Eaters" and other scenes depicting the hard lives of the peasantry and working poor.

I would like to revert to this setting and invite my readers to gather with me around this streetlight and let Nouwen speak to us in this book very informally as he did on that night in the auditorium at Yale. First he will tell us about himself. Then he will tell us about us.

He will tell us about himself through an interview he gave to *Critic* magazine in the summer of 1978, courtesy of Todd Brennan, of The Thomas More Association, who conducted the interview. Then he will begin telling us about us through letters which he wrote to his nineteen-year-old nephew, Marc, in the section to follow.

In his journal entry for May 1 in *Sabbatical Journey*, Nouwen relates an incident in which he is asked by his friend Frank Hamilton, a Presbyterian minister who is also an officer in the U.S. Air Force, if Henri would write a prayer for him on the occasion of his promotion. Nouwen relates his response to the request: "When I finally wrote the prayer, I felt drawn to make it a prayer that he [Frank] could pray, not only once but often. *I tried to crawl into his skin and speak to God from his heart.*"

The prayer can be found in the journal. The point to be made here is in the italic words: "I tried to crawl into his skin and speak to God from his heart." In those few words is found the secret of Nouwen's appeal to so many of his readers: his ability to identify, to crawl into the reader's skin, to offer a friendly space where readers can say in response: "You say what I suspected, you express what I vaguely felt, you bring to the fore what I fearfully kept in the back of my mind. Yes, yes—you say who we are, you recognize our condition…" (*Wounded Healer*, p. 39).

Deirdre LaNoue in her excellent study, *The Spiritual Legacy of Henri Nouwen* (see Bibliography, p. 138), sums up well the special appeal: "The value of a guide is found in his or her ability to meet you where you are, to understand how you got there, and to lead you to where you need to be." It is my hope that in the pages to follow I will be able to unleash something of that inspiring, enabling word that continues to speak to so many today.

I
SETTING

I never planned to be a writer
And have never really thought of myself
As a writer.
In fact my father always used to say
That I didn't have more than 300 words
In my vocabulary.

HENRI NOUWEN
CRITIC MAGAZINE, SUMMER 1978
INTERVIEW WITH TODD BRENNAN

AN INTERVIEW WITH HENRI NOUWEN

How I Got Started Writing

I never planned to be a writer and have never really thought of myself as a writer. In fact my father always used to say that I didn't have more than three hundred words in my vocabulary. It was quite accidental how I got started writing. I was asked to give a lecture to a conference of priests at Notre Dame. A stringer from the *National Catholic Reporter* sent the whole text to his paper and they printed it. There was an enormous response to the article. So I did more reflections and eventually they were put together in a book called *Intimacy*, which was published in 1969.

My next book, *Creative Ministry*, developed out of a process which is fairly representative of how I always work now. I came to Notre Dame to give a summer course, but after I arrived I found that the program had been canceled for lack of response. So, because they now had nothing for me to do, they asked me to give five lectures over the course of five weeks. I had nothing prepared but had a whole week to work on each lecture.

So I would choose a topic and then begin to talk with everyone about it. I decided not to go to the library to do research on the topic but instead just kept asking myself what I knew about it. What did I have available from my own experience? What did I know about it? Did I have some experience with this topic that I could articulate so that other people could recognize it as a real experience?

CRITIC MAGAZINE, SUMMER 1978,
INTERVIEW WITH TODD BRENNAN

My Prime Resource

So I have always used as my prime resource some of my own observations and my own personal struggles with whatever I am writing about. This is because I have always believed that one of the main objectives of ministry is to make your own faith struggles available to others, to articulate for others your own doubts and to say, in effect, "I don't know the answers either. I am simply a catalyst, simply somebody who wants to articulate for you things that you already know but might get a better grip on if there are some words for them." Later I might discuss with my associates and friends what other writers may have said about these things, but I think that my strength has always been starting from the shore of personal experience.

Then people start to respond. They begin to share their own experiences. And what they say helps me to distinguish between what is idiosyncratic—what are just Nouwen's personal ideas and experiences—and what touches a basic level of human experience. That's why I always keep in dialogue with people—many of my experiences are not necessarily normative or valuable for others.

CRITIC MAGAZINE, SUMMER 1978,
INTERVIEW WITH TODD BRENNAN

"Spiritual Life": What Does It Mean?

Spiritual life is the life of God's Spirit within us, both as individuals and as a community. Therefore the point of spiritual formation is to discern where something is happening. The reason for this is that there is a real tendency in us to think of the spiritual life as a life that will begin when we have certain feelings, think certain thoughts, or gain certain insights. The problem, however, is not how to make the spiritual life happen, but to see where it actually is happening. We work on the premise that God acts in this world, in the lives of individuals and communities. God is doing something. Our task is to become aware of where and how God is presently acting and to recognize that indeed it is God who is acting. Our task is to help people see that in fact they are involved in the spiritual life already.

Once this becomes visible, people can say, "Yes, God is already speaking to me, to us." Then, if we recognize God's claim on us, slowly our eyes are opened more and more and we begin to see what already has happened. We begin to see the greatness of God revealing itself in daily events, and our lives become a form of obedience.

Obedience means listening to and really hearing how much God loves us. Obedience means, therefore, slowly allowing God's Spirit to draw us to places some of which we might rather avoid. For God is a demanding God. God's love is a demanding love. God demands a lot of us, but he demands it out of love.

CRITIC MAGAZINE, SUMMER 1978,
INTERVIEW WITH TODD BRENNAN

God's Claim

The point is to say to people, "Let's explore where God's claim upon you has been made. Let's recognize it and say yes to the direction in which the Spirit calls you. The direction might be fearful at times or it might be quite radical, but you might also be surprised to see that the call of God in your life is a call that is very attractive and that you are able to do it because you are being drawn by a loving force."

So spiritual fulfillment in this sense is obviously a growing attentiveness to where God is in our life. It doesn't necessarily lead to tranquillity or to peace or to a beautiful feeling about each other or about how nice it is to be together. It might mean being lonely in a place where you never wanted to go. It may lead you to a vocation you had never sought. It might ask you to do uncomfortable things. Or it might ask you to do comfortable things that are not very dramatic. As Jesus said to Peter, "When you were young, you walked where you liked, but when you grow old somebody else will take

you where you would rather not go." And that means that
you end up on the Holy Cross. That's spiritual fulfillment.

CRITIC MAGAZINE, SUMMER 1978,
INTERVIEW WITH TODD BRENNAN

Teaching and Preaching

I think that real teaching and preaching should
create community, create a joyful recognition of being a
part of the same human condition. So I feel quite often
that the purpose of teaching or lecturing or preaching is
indeed to bring people together. It's a form of convening.
As a minister you are a convener.

So if I express something that others recognize as part of
their experience, then slowly they begin to recognize that
they are struggling with the same basic human questions
that I am. That's the process of recognition, of recognizing
that we are on the same paths, that we are all following the
same Lord and struggling with the same issues. And so
lecturing, teaching, and preaching create a community in
that people can say, "Yes, what you are talking about I can
connect with. It is not necessary that I have had exactly
the same experience. Rather I can make connections."

CRITIC MAGAZINE, SUMMER 1978,
INTERVIEW WITH TODD BRENNAN

Spirituality and Psychology

We are children of a psychological age. We are very
familiar with words such as conscious and unconscious,

depression and regression; frustration and defense mechanisms. Those words are used more frequently by students than words such as atonement, resurrection, sin, forgiveness, and grace. These words are much less existentially powerful than the psychological terminology. I, however, feel that if you simply remain in the psychological world, if you raise only psychological questions, you will get only psychological answers.

What I want to do is to show and make available the light of the Spirit, which is not necessarily the same as or bound to the psychological life, although there are endless interconnections. And I think it is very important for us to know psychological dynamics and know what depression and aggression and all of those things mean. But I would still like to say that spiritual dynamics cannot be reduced to or identified with these psychological dynamics. The Spirit blows where [it] wants to blow. It is precisely because of the freedom of the Spirit to heal us in wholly unexpected ways and to give us wholly unexpected possibilities for life that I would want to make a clear distinction—though not a separation—between spiritual direction and psychological counseling.

CRITIC MAGAZINE, SUMMER 1978,
INTERVIEW WITH TODD BRENNAN

Raising the Right Questions

One way I deal with this is by attempting to show students how to raise the right questions. (And once again I don't necessarily mean actually formulating questions.) So many of the questions that come out of life are expressed as psychological problems but are not necessarily so. Such questions need to be examined and even converted. Take, for instance, the question of how to cope with personal problems. There is a growing genre of literature in which simply coping with the problems of this or that stage of life becomes a central criterion of successful living. Now, the Christian could say that simple psychology could deal with these problems. But that is not the Good News. There is something about life you might not see if you depend only on psychology, something which gives the question about life's problems a completely different meaning.

Therefore, our task is not to deny the validity of the question that is shaped by the psychological perspective, but to say that there is a new level of questioning which opens up new perspectives and basically puts the question in a wholly different context, the context of God's reconciliation of the world in Jesus Christ.

CRITIC MAGAZINE, SUMMER 1978,
INTERVIEW WITH TODD BRENNAN

Hidden Expectations

People are...feeling a lot and they are suffering a lot, but it is so close to their own lives that it rarely comes up to the level of a question. And I don't even mean an intellectual question, but a question of any sort. But I think that this is where preaching, teaching, lecturing, and counseling come in. They are intended to help people create a friendly distance from their own lives so that what they are experiencing can be brought to light in the form of a question.

Let me give…a very simple example. Many people have a strong desire for intimacy, for closeness, for a sense of belonging, a sense of at-homeness, a sense of acceptance. This expresses itself on many levels—the way people express their love, the way they search for partners, the way people develop relationships and friendships, the way they sometimes stumble into marriages very quickly. When I preach, teach, lecture, or counsel, what is necessary first is for me to try to see where I recognize these feelings. It is not a matter of simply saying to myself that I can see what is happening to people. Rather it is a matter of looking at my own needs for intimacy and closeness and examining where these needs lead me.

And then slowly I begin to realize, for instance, that I really put claims on people that are so high that nobody can live up to them—emotional claims of which I was not even aware. I expect some person to take away my loneliness. I expect that person to give me a sense of at-homeness. I expect that when we live together everything will be joyful and pleasant.…

We have images in our heads about how things should be. And we don't always realize that these images and these expectations can cause an enormous amount of suffering because when people do not live up to these expectations, we can become not only disappointed but very vengeful, demanding, and angry. Many relationships break down because people have expectations of each other that are unrealistic. So it becomes clear that much of the violence between people is the result of false expectations. If we feel that others should give a great deal and they don't give it, then we might end up becoming very violent because our needs are great. We might go out into the streets or we might become very hardworking ambitious people who drive ourselves very hard to get this job or that salary. But what drives us may be a simple need for love. If we fail to recognize this simple need, we may end up in positions of wealth, power, or prestige and yet be very unhappy people.

I think first of all these things have to be made very visible. The task of the preacher or teacher is to say, "It's very painful to realize, but these are the conditions. I care for you. I don't expose this to you to hurt you but simply because I feel that it is something from which you are suffering. And may be suffering for the wrong reason. It is a type of suffering you don't need to have because it is based on a false expectation and understanding." The expectation is not an intellectual one but gut expectation.

And when, on the basis of that encounter, people slowly start to recognize how parents, children, husbands and wives, employers and employees, are all suffering, quite often because of these expectations, then they may understand what is meant in the Gospel when it is said that we can only love because we have been loved first.

CRITIC MAGAZINE, SUMMER 1978, INTERVIEW WITH TODD BRENNAN

*L*ETTERS TO MARC ABOUT JESUS

*I*n the preface to his book, Letters to Marc About Jesus, Nouwen explains how he came to publish these letters written to his nephew in the Netherlands, Marc van Campen. Nouwen had been approached for a number of years by a Dutch publisher, asking that Nouwen write a book in his native tongue. With the exception of two of his earliest books, Nouwen's books were always written and published in English, since he had established residency in the United States. Nouwen's response to the Dutch publisher was that he had been living in the U.S. so long and spent so little time in his native country that he felt he was in no position to sense and respond in an informed manner to the mental climate in the Netherlands.

The Dutch publisher was not easily put off. As an alternative he suggested that Nouwen write a series of letters to someone in his native land to whom he could at least convey something of his own convictions about the spiritual life as he was living it in his new environment. Nouwen found this new proposal appealing and approached his nephew to ask if he would be willing to participate in the project. The nephew was happy to accommodate, and out of this arrangement come

Letters to Marc About Jesus, *originally written in Dutch and subsequently published in English.*

Nouwen takes pains to make clear in his introduction, that though his thoughts are expressed in the form of letters to his nephew, he was careful to keep in mind, once he agreed to the project, that he was in fact writing for publication and hence, speaking to a much broader readership. As I began the task of combing the writings of Henri Nouwen in search for passages I might wish to include in this collection, I was struck by one passage in particular. In Letter Number 4, Nouwen describes to his nephew the situation he finds when he visits his native Holland. He finds people who are better off financially, but he also notices that increasing prosperity has not made people more friendly toward one another: "I get the impression that people are more preoccupied with themselves and have less time for one another than when they didn't possess so much." He finds people have less opportunity to relax, to get together informally and enjoy the little things in life: "It seems sometimes as though meetings between people generally happen on the way to something or someone else."

When I read these lines, I thought to myself: How much this sounds like life right here in the United States! What is our condition today, as we cross the threshold of the twenty-first century? I think Nouwen describes it well in his Letters to Marc About Jesus. It is for this reason that I have chosen to make the Letters my point of departure in laying out the design of the rest of the book. Again I remind the reader: Nouwen is speaking not only to his nineteen-year-old nephew. He is speaking to us. He is telling us about us. The letters speak to all ages.

Price of Success

As you know, I come to the Netherlands only occasionally and so changes strike me more forcibly than if I were living there all the time. I have noticed one thing in particular: increasing prosperity has not made people more friendly toward one another. They're better off; but that newfound wealth has not resulted in a new sense of community. I get the impression that people are more preoccupied with themselves and have less time for one another than when they didn't possess so much. There's more competitiveness, more envy, more unrest, and more anxiety. There's less opportunity to relax, to get together informally, and enjoy the little things in life. Success has isolated a lot of people and made them lonely.

LETTERS TO MARC, LETTER IV

Under the Blanket of Success

Is it so astonishing, then, that in the Netherlands as in other prosperous countries there are so many people who are lonely, depressed, and anxious and are never genuinely happy? At times, I get the feeling that, under the blanket of success, a lot of people fall asleep in tears. And the question that perhaps lies hidden most deeply in many hearts is the question of love. "Who really cares about me? Not about my money, my contacts, my reputation, or my popularity but just me? Where do I really feel at home, secure, and cherished? Where can I freely say and think what I like without the fear of losing out on love? Where am I really safe"

LETTERS TO MARC, LETTER IV

Relationships As Trading Markets

The most important thing you can say about God's love is that God loves us not because of anything we've done to earn that love, but because God, in total freedom, has decided to love us. At first sight, this doesn't seem to be very inspiring; but if you reflect on it more deeply this thought can affect and influence your life greatly. We're inclined to see our whole existence in terms of quid pro quo. We assume that people will be nice to us if we are nice to them; that they will help us if we help them; that they will invite us if we invite them; that they will love us if we love them. And so the conviction is deeply rooted in us that being loved is something you have to earn. In our pragmatic and utilitarian times this conviction has become even stronger. We can scarcely conceive of getting something for nothing. Everything has to be worked for, even a kind word, an expression of gratitude, a sign of affection.

LETTERS TO MARC, LETTER V

High Price of Recognition

I think it's this mentality that lies behind a lot of anxiety, unrest, and agitation. It's as though we're forever on the go, trying to prove to each other that we deserve to be loved. The doubt we harbor within us drives us on to ever-greater activity. In that way we try to keep our heads above water and not drown in our ever-increasing lack of self-respect. The enormous propensity to seek recognition, admiration, popularity, and renown is rooted in the fear that without all this we are worthless. You could call it the "commercialization" of love. Nothing for nothing. Not even love.

LETTERS TO MARC, LETTER V

When Kissing Turns Into Biting

The tragic thing, though, is that we humans aren't capable of dispelling one another's loneliness and lack of self-respect....Our ability to satisfy one another's deepest longing is so limited that time and time again we are in danger of disappointing one another. Despite all this, at times our longing can be so intense that it blinds us to our mutual limitations and we are led into the temptation of extorting love, even when reason tells us that we can't give one another any total, unlimited, unconditional love. It is then that love becomes violent. It is then that kisses become bites, caresses become blows, forgiving looks become suspicious glances, lending a sympathetic ear becomes eavesdropping, and heartfelt surrender becomes violation. The borderline between love and force is frequently transgressed, and in our anxiety-ridden times it doesn't take very much to let our desire for love lead us to violent behavior.

LETTERS TO MARC, LETTER V

Where to Find Noncoercive, Nonviolent Love?

When I look about me and see the many forms of coercion present in human relationships, I often have a sense of seeing here, there, and everywhere people who want nothing more or less than to be loved, but who have been unable to find any way to express that longing other than through violence, either to others or to themselves. I sometimes get the impression that our prisons are crammed full of people who couldn't express their need to be loved except by flailing about furiously and hurting others. At the same time, many of our psychiatric institutions are filled with people who, full of shame and guilt, have given a form to the self-same need by inflicting damage on themselves. Whether we do violence to others or to ourselves, what we long for in our heart is a nonviolent, peaceful communion in which we know ourselves to be secure and loved. But how and where are we to find that noncoercive, nonviolent love?

LETTERS TO MARC, LETTER V

Love's True North

In what I've been describing as coercive love, you will, I hope, have detected something of yourself or of the people around you. If so, you will the more readily understand what Jesus means when he speaks of love. Jesus is the revelation of God's unending, unconditional love for us human beings. Everything that Jesus has done, said, and undergone is meant to show us that the love we most long for is given to us by God—not being we've deserved it but because God is a God of love.

Jesus shows us that true love, the love that comes from God, makes no distinction between friends and foes, between people who are for us and people who are against us, people who do us a favor and people who do us ill. God makes no such distinction. He loves all human beings, good or bad, with the same unconditional love. This all-embracing love Jesus offers to us, and he invites us to make this love visible in our lives.

LETTERS TO MARC, LETTER V

Claiming Our True Home

If our love, like God's, embraces friend as well as foe, we have become children of God and are no longer children of suspicion, jealousy, violence, war, and death. Our love for our enemies shows to whom we really belong. It shows our true home. Jesus states it so clearly: "…love your enemies, and do good to them, and lend without any hope of return. You will have a great reward, and you will be children of the Most High, for he himself is kind to the ungrateful and the wicked."

LETTERS TO MARC, LETTER V

A New Way of Being Human

There you have it: the love of God is an unconditional love, and only that love can empower us to live together without violence. When we know that God loves us deeply and will always go on loving us, whoever we are and whatever we do, it becomes possible to expect no more of our fellow men and women than they are able to give, to forgive them generously when they have offended us, and to respond to their hostility with love. By doing so we make visible a new way of being human and a new way of responding to our world problems.

LETTERS TO MARC, LETTER V

God Revealed in Hiddenness

There was nothing spectacular about Jesus' life—far from it! Even when you look at Jesus' miracles, you find that he did not heal or call back to life people in order to get publicity. He frequently forbade them even to talk about it. His resurrection too was a hidden event. Only his disciples and a few of the women and men who had known him well before his death were allowed to see him as the risen Lord.

Now that Christianity has become one of the major world religions and millions of people utter the name of Jesus every day, it's hard for us to believe that Jesus revealed God in hiddenness. But neither Jesus' life nor his death, nor his resurrection were intended to astound us with the great power of God. God became a lowly, hidden, almost invisible God.

I'm constantly struck by the fact that wherever the gospel of Jesus bears fruit, we come across this hiddenness. The great Christians throughout history have always been lowly people who sought to be hidden. Benedict hid himself in the vale of Subiaco, Francis in the Carceri outside Assisi, Ignatius in the grotto of Manresa, and the little Thérèse in the Carmel of Lisieux. Whenever you hear about saintly people, you sense a deep longing for that hiddenness, that seclusion. We so easily forget it, but Paul too withdrew into the wilderness for two years before he started on his preaching mission.

LETTERS TO MARC, LETTER VI

Secret Lives in an Age of Publicity

The initial reaction of someone who has a really personal encounter with Jesus is not to start shouting it from the rooftops, but to dwell secretly in the presence of God. It is very important for you to realize that perhaps the greater part of God's work in this world may go unnoticed. There are a number of people who in these days have become widely known as great saints or influential Christians: Mother Teresa in Calcutta, Bishop Romero in El Salvador, Padre Pio in Italy, and Dorothy Day in New York, but the greatest part of God's work in our history could well remain completely unknown.

That's a mystery which is difficult to grasp in an age that attaches so much value to publicity.

LETTERS TO MARC, LETTER VI

Notoriety, Money, and Power

We tend to think that the more people know and talk about something the more important it must be. That is understandable considering the fact that great notoriety often means big money, and big money often means a large amount of power, and power easily creates the illusion of importance. In our society it is often statistics that determine what's important: the best-selling record, the most popular book, the richest man, the highest building, the most expensive car. With the enormous spread and growth of advertising, it's become nearly impossible to believe that what's really important happens in secret. Yet . . . we do possess some intimations of this.

LETTERS TO MARC, LETTER VI

Intimacy Needs Seclusion

A human life begins in the seclusion of the womb, and the most determinative experiences occur in the privacy of the family. The seedling grows in the seclusion of the soil, and the egg is hatched in the seclusion of the nest. Like creativity, intimacy too needs seclusion. We know intuitively that everything which moves us by its delicacy, vulnerability, and pristine beauty can stand only very little public exposure. The mass media, which magnify creativity and intimacy, are proof of that. What is precious and sacred in hiddenness often becomes cheap and even vulgar when exposed to the public by the mass media. Publicity standardizes, hardens, and not infrequently suffocates what it exposes.

LETTERS TO MARC, LETTER VI

Unmasking the Big Lie

Many great minds and spirits have lost their creative force through too early or too rapid exposure to the public. We know it; we sense it; but we easily forget it because our world persists in proclaiming the big lie: "Being unknown means being unloved." If you're ready to trust your intuition and so preserve a degree of healthy skepticism in the face of the current propaganda, you are more likely to detect the hidden presence of God.

LETTERS TO MARC, LETTER VI

Strangers in Our Own House

And here we're back again with the mystery of our own heart. Our heart is at the center of our being human. There our deepest thoughts, intuitions, emotions, and decisions find their source. But it's also there that we are most alienated from ourselves. We know little or nothing of our heart. We keep our distance from it, as though we were afraid of it. What is most intimate is also what frightens us most. Where we are most ourselves, we are often strangers to ourselves. That is the painful part of our being human. We fail to know our hidden center; and so we live and die often without knowing who we really are. If we ask ourselves why we think, feel, and act in a certain way, we often have no answer, thus proving to be strangers in our own house.

LETTERS TO MARC, LETTER VI

A Meeting Place for the Human and Divine

The discipline of the heart helps us to let God into our hearts and become known to us there, in the deepest recesses of our own being. This is not so easy to do; we like to be master in our own house and don't want to admit that our house is God's house too. God wants to be together with us where we really live and, by loving us there, show us the way to become a complete human being. God's love is a demanding love, even a jealous love; and when we let that love speak within us, we are led into places where we often would rather not go.

And yet we know that everyone who has allowed God's love to enter into his or her heart has not only become a better human being, but has also contributed significantly to making a better world. The lives of the saints show us that. And so I say, make room in your heart for God and let God cherish you. There you can be alone with God. There heart speaks to heart and there in that holy seclusion the new person will be born in you.

LETTERS TO MARC, LETTER VI

II
$\mathscr{A}$WARENESS

People expect too much
from speaking,
too little from silence . . ..

GENESEE DIARY

Words can only bear fruit
when they are born in silence.

CLOWNING IN ROME

SILENCE

How We Avoid Silence

For many, silence is threatening. They don't know what to do with it. If they leave the noise of the city behind and come upon a place where no cars are roaring by, no ships tooting, no trains rumbling; where there is no hum of radio or television, where no CDs or tapes are playing, they feel their entire bodies gripped by an intense unrest. They feel like a fish thrown on dry land. They have lost their bearings. Some people can't study without a solid wall of music surrounding them. If they are forced to sit in a room without a constant flow of sound, they grow very nervous.

WITH OPEN HANDS

Noise As Normal

Thus, for many of us, silence has become a threat. There was a time when silence was normal, and a lot of noise disturbed us. But today, noise is the normal fare, and silence—strange as it may seem—has become the disturbance. It is not hard to understand that people who experience silence in this way have difficulty with prayer.

WITH OPEN HANDS

Sounds of Silence

We have become alienated from silence. If we go to the beach or on a picnic in the woods, the Walkman is often our most important companion. It seems that we can't bear the sound of silence.

Silence is full of sounds: the wind murmuring, the leaves rustling, the birds flapping their wings, the waves washing ashore. And even if these sounds cannot be heard, we still hear our own quiet breathing, the motion of our hands over our skin, the swallowing in our throats, and the soft patter of our footsteps. But we have become deaf to these sounds of silence.

When we are invited to move from our noisy world into this sound-filled silence, we often become frightened. We feel like children who see the walls of a house collapse and suddenly find themselves in an open field, or we feel as though we have been violently stripped of our clothing, or like birds torn away from their nests. Our ears begin to ache because the familiar noise is missing; and our bodies have become used to that noise as if it were a down blanket keeping us warm. We become like addicts who must go through the painful process of withdrawal.

WITH OPEN HANDS

Confronting the Noise Inside

*B*ut still more difficult than getting rid of these exterior noises is the achievement of inner silence, a silence of the heart. It seems that a person who is caught up in all that noise has lost touch with the inner self. The questions which are asked from within remain unanswered. Unsure feelings are not cleared up; tangled desires are not straightened out, and confusing emotions are not understood. All that remains is a chaotic tumble of feelings which have never had a chance to be sorted out.

It is hardly surprising, then, that when we shut off all the daily racket, a new inner noise can often be heard, rising from all those chaotic feelings screaming for attention. Entering into a quiet room doesn't automatically bring us inner silence. When there is no one to talk to or to listen to, an interior discussion may start up—often noisier than the noise we just escaped. Many unsolved problems demand attention; one care forces itself upon the other; one complaint rivals the next; all pleading for a hearing. Sometimes we are left powerless in the face of the many twisted sentiments we cannot untangle. It makes you wonder if the diversion we look for in the many things outside us might not be an attempt to avoid a confrontation with what is inside.

WITH OPEN HANDS

SOLITUDE

Creating a Space for God

*W*ithout solitude it is virtually impossible to live a spiritual life. Solitude begins with a time and place for God, and God alone. If we really believe not only that God exists but also that God is actively present in our lives—healing, teaching, and guiding—we need to set aside a time and space to give God our undivided attention. Jesus says, "Go to your private room and, when you have shut your door, pray to your Father who is in that secret place" (Mt 6:6).

To bring some solitude into our lives is one of the most necessary but also most difficult disciplines. Even though we may have a deep desire for real solitude, we also experience a certain apprehension as we approach that solitary place and time. As soon as we are alone, without people to talk with, books to read, TV to watch, or phone calls to make, an inner chaos opens up in us. This chaos can be so disturbing and so confusing that we can hardly wait to get busy again. Entering a private room and shutting the door, therefore, does not mean that we immediately shut out all our inner doubts, anxieties, fears, bad memories, unresolved conflicts, angry feelings, and impulsive desires. On the contrary, when we have removed our outer distractions, we often find that our inner distractions manifest themselves to us in full force. We often use the outer distractions to shield ourselves from the interior noises. It is thus not surprising that we have a difficult time being alone.

Solitude is not a spontaneous response to an occupied and preoccupied life. There are too many reasons not to be alone. Therefore we must begin by carefully planning some solitude. Five or ten minutes a day may be all we can tolerate. Perhaps we are ready for an hour every day, an afternoon every week, a day every month, or a week every year. The amount of time will vary for each person according to temperament, age, job, lifestyle, and maturity. But we do not take the spiritual life seriously if we do not set aside some time to be with God and listen to him.

MAKING ALL THINGS NEW

Living With Open Doors

Once we have committed ourselves to spending time in solitude, we develop an attentiveness to God's voice in us. In the beginning, during the first days, weeks, or even months, we may have the feeling that we are simply wasting our time. Time in solitude may at first seem little more than a time in which we are bombarded by thousands of thoughts and feelings that emerge from hidden areas of our mind. One of the early Christian writers describes the first stage of solitary prayer as the experience of a man who, after years of living with open doors, suddenly decides to shut them. The visitors who used to come and enter his home start pounding on his doors, wondering why they are not allowed to enter. Only when they realize that they are not welcome do they gradually stop coming. This is the experience of anyone who decides to enter into solitude after a life without much spiritual discipline. At first, the many distractions keep presenting themselves. Later, as they receive less and less attention, they slowly withdraw.

The discipline of solitude, as I have described it here, is one of the most powerful disciplines in developing a prayerful life. It is a simple, though not easy, way to free us from the slavery of our occupations and preoccupations and to begin to hear the voice that makes all things new.

MAKING ALL THINGS NEW

The Wagon Wheel

In my home country, the Netherlands, you will see many large wagon wheels, not on wagons, but as decorations at the entrances of farms or on the walls of restaurants. I have always been fascinated by these wagon wheels: with their wide rims, strong wooden spokes, and big hubs. These wheels help me to understand the importance of a life lived from the center. When I move along the rim, I can reach one spoke after the other, but when I stay at the hub, I am in touch with all the spokes at once.

HERE AND NOW

Moving to the Center

To pray is to move to the center of all life and all love. The closer I come to the hub of life, the closer I come to all that receives its strength and energy from there. My tendency is to get so distracted by the diversity of the many spokes of life, that I am busy but not truly life-giving, all over the place but not focused. By directing my attention to the heart of life, I am connected with its rich variety while remaining centered. What does the hub represent? I think of it as my own heart, the heart of God, and the heart of the world. When I pray, I enter into the depth of my own heart and find there the heart of God, who speaks to me of love. And I recognize, right there, the place where all of my sisters and brothers are in communion with one another. The great paradox of the spiritual life is, indeed, that the most personal is most universal, that the most intimate, is most communal, and that the most contemplative is most active.

The wagon wheel shows that the hub is the center of all energy and movement, even when it often seems not to be moving at all. In God all action and all rest are one. So too prayer!

HERE AND NOW

PRAYER

The Bridge of Prayer

Prayer is the bridge between my unconscious and conscious self. Prayer connects my mind with my heart, my will with my passions, my brain with my belly. Prayer is the way to let the life-giving Spirit of God penetrate all the corners of my being. Prayer is the divine instrument of my wholeness, unity and inner peace.

SABBATICAL JOURNEY

Listening to the Blessing

For me personally, prayer becomes more and more a listening to the blessing. I have read and written much about prayer, but when I go to a quiet place to pray, I realize that, although I have a tendency to say many things to God, the real "work" of prayer is to become silent and listen to the voice that says good things about me. This might sound self-indulgent, but, in practice, it is a hard discipline. I am so afraid of being cursed, of hearing that I am no good or not good enough, that I quickly give in to the temptation to start talking and to keep talking in order to control my fears. To gently push aside and silence the many voices that question my goodness and to trust that I will hear a voice of blessing...that demands real effort.

Have you ever tried to spend a whole hour doing nothing but listening to the voice that dwells deep in your heart? When there is no radio to listen to, no TV to watch, no book to read, no person to talk to, no project to finish, no phone call to make, how does that make you feel? Often it does no more than make us so aware of how much there is still to do that we haven't yet done that we decide to leave the fearful silence and go back to work! It is not easy to enter into the silence and reach beyond the many boisterous and demanding voices of our world and to discover there the small intimate voice saying: "You are my Beloved Child, on you my favor rests." Still, if we dare to embrace our solitude and befriend our silence, we will come to know that voice. I do not want to suggest to you that one day you will hear that voice with your bodily ears. I am not speaking about a hallucinatory voice, but about a voice that can be heard by the ear of faith, the ear of the inner heart.

Often you will feel that nothing happens in your prayer. You say: "I am just sitting there and getting distracted." But if you develop the discipline of spending one half-hour a day listening to the voice of love, you will gradually discover that something is happening of which you were not even conscious. It might be only in retrospect that you discover the voice that blesses you.

You thought that what happened during your time of listening was nothing more than a lot of confusion, but then you discover yourself looking forward to your quiet time and missing it when you can't have it. The movement of God's Spirit is very gentle, very soft—and hidden. It does not seek attention. But that movement is also very persistent, strong and deep. It changes our hearts radically. The faithful discipline of prayer reveals to you that you are the blessed one and gives you the power to bless others.

LIFE OF THE BELOVED

Prayer of Abandonment

This morning during my hour of prayer, I tried to come to some level of abandonment to my heavenly Father. It was a hard struggle since so much in me wants to do my will, realize my plans, organize my future, and make my decisions. Still, I know that true joy comes from letting God love me the way God wants, whether it is through illness or health, failure or success, poverty or wealth, rejection or praise. It is hard for me to say, "I shall gratefully accept everything, Lord, that pleases you. Let your will be done." But I know that when I truly believe my Father is pure love, it will become increasingly possible to say these words from the heart.

Charles de Foucauld once wrote a prayer of abandonment that expresses beautifully the spiritual attitude I wish I had. Sometimes I pray it, even though

the words do not yet fully come from my heart. I will
write them down here:

> Father,
> I abandon myself into your hands;
> do with me what you will.
> Whatever you may do, I thank you;
> I am ready for all, I accept all.
> Let only your will be done in me
> and in all your creatures.
> I wish no more than this,
> O Lord.
> Into your hands I commend my soul;
> I offer it to you with all the love
> of my heart,
> for I love you, Lord,
> and so need to give myself,
> to surrender myself into your hands,
> without reserve
> and with boundless confidence.
> For you are my Father.

It seems good to pray this prayer often. These are the
words of a holy man, and they show the way I must go. I
realize that I can never make this prayer come true by my
own efforts. But the spirit of Jesus given to me can help
me pray it and grow to its fulfillment. I know that my
inner peace depends on my willingness to make this
prayer my own.

THE ROAD TO DAYBREAK

Evening Prayer in the Monastery

The evening prayers called Compline (meaning: to make the day complete) form one of the most intimate moments of the monastic day. It is the moment during which all the monks are present, even those who sometimes have to be absent during other prayers, and during which you sense a real togetherness. The prayers are always the same. Therefore, nobody needs a book. Everyone can stand wherever he wants, and therefore no lights are necessary. All is quiet in the house. It is the beginning of what the monks call the great silence which lasts from 6:30 P.M. until 5:30 A.M.

Compline is such an intimate and prayerful moment that some people in the neighborhood come daily to the abbey to join in this most quiet prayer of the day.

I start realizing that the psalms of Compline slowly become flesh in me; they become part of my night and lead me to a peaceful sleep.

Ponder on your bed and be still:
Make justice your sacrifice and trust in the Lord.
I will lie down in peace
and sleep comes at once for You alone, Lord,
make me dwell in safety (Ps 4).

Trust is written all through the evening prayer:

> He who dwells in the shelter of the Most High
> and abides in the shade of the Almighty says to
> the Lord: "My refuge, my stronghold, my God
> in whom I trust!"
>
> It is he who will free you from the snare of
> the fowler who seeks to destroy you; he will
> conceal you with his pinions and under his
> wings you will find refuge (Ps 90).

Slowly these words enter into the center of my heart. They are more than ideas, images, comparisons: They become a real presence. After a day with much work or with many tensions, you feel that you can let go in safety and realize how good it is to dwell in the shelter of the Most High.

Many times I have thought: If I am ever sent to prison, if I am ever subjected to hunger, pain, torture, or humiliation, I hope and pray that they let me keep the psalms. The psalms will keep my spirit alive, the psalms will allow me to comfort others, the psalms will prove the most powerful, yes, the most revolutionary weapon against the oppressor and torturer. How happy are those who no longer need books but carry the psalms in their heart wherever they are and wherever they go. Maybe I should start learning the psalms by heart so that nobody can take them away from me. Just to be able to say over and over again:

O men, how long will your hearts be closed,
will you love what is futile and seek what is
false?

It is the Lord who grants favors to those
whom he loves; the Lord hears me whenever
I call him (Ps 4).

GENESEE DIARY

The Psalms by Heart

Once in a while I see a monk reading from a small
pocket book of the psalms while doing something else
(stirring soup, for instance). I know that he is trying to
memorize the psalms. I recently read a letter written by a
Trappistine sister in which she wrote that she knew more
than half of the one hundred fifty psalms by heart. What
a gift to be able to pray those words at any time and at
any place. I can understand better now how they can give
us eagles' wings and renew constantly our strength.

GENESEE DIARY

A Protective Presence

Gradually I am becoming aware of a new dimension
in my prayer life. It is hard to find words for it, but it feels
like a protective presence of God, Mary, the angels and
the saints that exists in the midst of distractions, fears,
temptations, and inner confusion.

While my prayers were not at all intensive or

profound, I had a real desire to spend time in prayer this week. I enjoyed just sitting in the small dark side chapel of the mother house of the Vincentian Sisters. I felt surrounded by goodness, gentleness, kindness, and acceptance. I felt as if angels' wings were keeping me safe: a protective cloud covering me and keeping me there. Though it is very hard to express, this new experience is the experience of being protected against the dangers of a seductive world.

But this protection is very soft, gentle, caring. Not the protection of a wall or a metal screen. It is more like a hand on my shoulder or a kiss on my forehead. But for all this protection, I am not taken away from the dangers. I am not lifted from the seductive world. I am not removed from violence, hatred, lust, and greed. In fact, I feel them in the center of my being, screaming for my full attention. They are restless and noisy. Still, this hand, these lips, these eyes are present and I know that I am safe, held in love, cared for, and protected by the good spirits of heaven.

So I am praying while not knowing how to pray. I am resting while feeling restless, at peace while tempted, safe while still anxious, surrounded by a cloud of light while still in darkness, in love while still doubting.

The Road to Daybreak

Real Prayer

True prayer always includes becoming poor.

Gracias! A Latin American Journal

III
RESPONSE

*I still believe deeply that our few years on this earth
are part of a much larger event that stretches out
far beyond the boundaries of our birth and death.
I think of it as a mission into time
a mission that is very exhilarating and even exciting,
Mostly because the One who sent me on the mission
Is waiting for me to come home and tell the story
of what I have learned.*

HENRI J. M. NOUWEN, *LIFE OF THE BELOVED*

CONTEMPLATION AND ACTION

Prayer and Television

Last night I watched a television conversation between Bill Moyers and Joseph Campbell. It was a rerun of a series of programs made in the eighties. I was struck by Campbell's remark that we serve the world by being spiritually well. The first questions are not: "How much do we do?" or "How many people do we help out?" but "Are we interiorly at peace?" Campbell confirmed my own conviction that the distinction between contemplation and action can be misleading. Jesus' actions flowed from his interior communion with God. His presence was healing, and it changed the world. In a sense he didn't do anything! "Everyone who touched him was healed" (Mk 6:56).

This morning during the Eucharist we discussed the great commandment. The same theme came up. When we love God with all our heart, mind, strength, and soul, we cannot do other than love our neighbor, and our very selves. It is by being fully rooted in the heart of God that we are creatively connected with our neighbor as well as with our deepest self. In the heart of God we can see that the other human beings who live on this earth with us are also God's son and daughters, and belong to the same family we do. There too I can recognize and claim my own belovedness, and celebrate it with my neighbors.

Our society thinks economically: "How much love do I give to God, how much to my neighbor, and how much to myself?" But God says, "Give all your love to me, and I will give you your neighbor and yourself." We are not talking here about moral obligations or ethical imperatives. We are talking about the mystical life. It is the intimate communion with God that reveals to us how to live in the world and act in God's Name.

I keep wondering if it is wise for me to get so involved with television. I never watch TV and hardly see the programs that I am part of. Still, it is a powerful medium. What irritates me most about TV is that the visual so dominates the audio. People say, "Oh, I saw you on TV. I liked your enthusiasm and the way you used your hands." When I ask, "What did you think about the ideas we discussed?" they seldom have a response.

SABBATICAL JOURNEY

We Become What We See

I am reading a fascinating chapter from Jerry Mander's book, *Four Arguments for the Elimination of Television*. The main idea is: "We evolve into the images we carry in our minds. We become what we see. And in today's America, what most of us see is one hell of a lot of television."

I had heard stories about Vietnam veterans who, during their first real battle, thought that it was just another war movie and were shocked when those they killed did not stand up and walk away. I had read that Vincent van Gogh saw the real world as an imitation of the paintings he saw in the museum. I had noticed how children often are more excited about the repeated advertisements on television than about the movie they interrupt. But I had never fully thought through the enormous impact of the artificially imposed images on my thoughts, feelings, and actions. When it is true that the image you carry in your mind can affect your physical, mental, and emotional life, then it becomes a crucial question as to which images we expose ourselves or allow ourselves to be exposed.

GRACIAS! A LATIN AMERICAN JOURNAL

Our True Identity

All of this is important to me because it has profound spiritual implications. Prayer also has much to do with imagining. When I bring myself into the presence of God, I imagine God in many ways as a loving father, a supporting sister, a caring mother, a severe teacher, an honest judge, a fellow traveler, an intimate friend, a gentle healer, a challenging leader, a demanding taskmaster. All these "personalities" create images in my mind that affect not only what I think but also how I actually experience myself. I believe that true prayer makes us into what we imagine. To pray to God leads to becoming like God….Divinization is, indeed, the goal of all prayer and meditation. This divinization allows Saint Paul to say: "I live now not with my own life but with the life of Christ who lives in me" (Gal 2:20).

The more we come to depend on the images offered to us by those who try to distract us, entertain us, use us for their purposes, and make us conform to the demands of a consumer society, the easier it is for us to lose our identity. These imposed images actually make us into the world which they represent, a world of hatred, violence, lust, greed, manipulation, and oppression. But when we believe that we are created in the image of God and come to realize that Christ came to let us reimagine this, then meditation and prayer can lead us to our true identity.

GRACIAS! A LATIN AMERICAN JOURNAL

WORDS AND ACTIONS

The Word Made Flesh

The most important question for me is not, "How do I touch people?" but, "How do I live the word I am speaking?" In Jesus, no division existed between his words and his actions, between what he said and what he did. Jesus' words were his action, his words were events. They not only spoke about changes, cures, new life, but they actually created them. In this sense, Jesus is truly the Word made flesh; in that Word all is created and by that Word all is re-created. Saintliness means living without division between word and action. If I would truly live in my own life the word I am speaking, my spoken words would become actions, and miracles would happen whenever I opened my mouth.

GRACIAS! A LATIN AMERICAN JOURNAL

Connectedness

Jesus describes the intimacy that he offers as the connectedness between the vine and its branches. I long to be grafted onto Jesus as a branch onto the vine so that all my life comes from the vine. In communion with

Jesus, the vine, my little life can grow and bear fruit....My
true spiritual work is to let myself be loved, fully and
completely, and to trust that in that love I will come to
the fulfillment of my vocation.

SABBATICAL JOURNEY

Mysticism:
The Opposite of Withdrawal

With great interest I read Evelyn Underhill's *The
Mystics of the Church*. In this book Underhill discusses in
a very lively and incisive way the main mystical figures in
the Western Church. It is one of the most convincing
arguments for the Christian belief that the love of God
lived in its fullest sense leads to a most selfless dedication
to the neighbor. Underhill shows how, after living through
the most ecstatic experiences, the mystics are frequently
capable of unbelievable activity. Paul is the prime example,
but Augustine, Teresa of Ávila, Catherine of Siena, and
many others show the same capacity. Mysticism is the
opposite of withdrawal from the world. Intimate union
with God leads to the most creative involvement in the
contemporary world. It seems that ecstasies and visions are
slowly replaced by a "steady inward certainty of union
with God and by a new strength and endurance." Although
frequently experiencing "sudden waves of fervent feelings"
in this often very active period, the mystic is "nonetheless
calm and sober in his practical dealings with men."

GENESEE DIARY

RESPONSE—PART 3

*W*HY AREN'T
YOU IN SELMA?

*O*n March 7, 1965, a historic civil rights march from
Selma to Montgomery, Alabama, was blocked at the Edmund
Pettis Bridge outside Selma. Police used tear gas and beat the
unarmed marchers with clubs, injuring one hundred and forty
people. In response, Martin Luther King, Jr., called upon
church leaders and people of faith from around the country to
come immediately to Selma for a second march to Montgomery, which began on March 21, 1965. Henri Nouwen was
studying at the Menninger Clinic in Topeka, Kansas, at the
time and decided to join the civil rights march.

ROAD TO PEACE

From Topeka
to Selma to Montgomery

*I*t all began with a feeling of restlessness, an inner
compulsion, a fierce gnawing, a painful question: Why
aren't you in Selma? You talk about integration, you say
that it's more than a national problem, you believe in the
right of men and women to be free, but you're not in
Selma. No time, no money, or no courage?

Seldom have I felt this inner restlessness so strongly than after Martin Luther King made his appeal to his people to help in the struggle for freedom. And seldom have there been so many people coming up with excuses for not going. "It's a local affair and it's not up to you to interfere, especially since you are a foreigner." "You're looking for thrills and excitement; better to do your duty where you are instead of running off to a problem for which you can't possibly bear any lasting responsibility." But the restlessness wouldn't go away; it even increased as the days passed.

ROAD TO PEACE

Which Side Are You On, Boy?

I'm not one for demonstrations. I've never had much sympathy for the people who march down the streets of London or Amsterdam. But this seemed different. It became difficult to sleep, to eat, and to work. That question kept hounding me: Why aren't you in Selma?

I knew that they had already left. On Sunday, March 21, they had once again crossed the bridge over the Alabama River. Two weeks after being cruelly beaten by the state troopers they were back, but this time there were thousands of them, determined to complete the fifty miles to Montgomery. I knew that the song had been sung ten, a hundred, a thousand times:

Which side are you on, boy?
Which side are you on?
With billy clubs they slew us down,
they hit us with a cane.
But we came back with thousands more
and walked our way again.
Which side are you on, boy?
Which side are you on?

ROAD TO PEACE

Midnight Rider

On Sunday, March 28, at eleven o'clock at night,
tossing and turning in my bed, I suddenly knew that I had
made a mistake. With alarming certainty I realized that I
still had four days to undo the damage. That was when I
made my decision. By midnight I was in my Volkswagen,
driving out of Topeka, Kansas, and heading for the South,
the deep, deep South. A remarkable change took place.
The restlessness disappeared, and there was a deep,
palpable certainty and sense of determination. No fatigue,
no sleep. I trained my eyes on the endless roads of Kansas,
flooring it, fast and sure.

From Kansas to Oklahoma, from Oklahoma to
Arkansas, from Arkansas to Louisiana, from Louisiana to
Mississippi, from Mississippi to Alabama. Every now and
then I'd get a few hours' sleep in a highway motel and
then head another thousand miles farther, down to
Selma.

ROAD TO PEACE

Charles

In Vicksburg, Mississippi, there was a black man standing by the roadside, keeping a safe and rather timid distance from the roadway. Charles, age twenty, my first friend. After climbing into the car he said, "God has heard my prayer. He sent you as an angel from heaven. I've been standing here for hours and nobody would pick me up. The white man only wants to run at me and push me off the road. When you hitchhike you take your life in your hands, but I want to go to Selma. I made a cross in the sand with my stick, and I prayed to God that he would bring me to Selma to help my people. He heard my prayer." As we drove through the night Charles told me about the dark days of Mississippi.

He'd been imprisoned five times in his fight for freedom. He'd demonstrated with thousands of others, for the integration of schools, courts, restaurants, and shops. "Never go alone. Go with thousands. The more there are in jail the sooner you'll get out. They have to feed you, and that's expensive; they have to have room for you, and that's scarce; they need guards and there aren't enough. Go with thousands. That'll cost them money and they'll just have to release you."

He told me about the murder of his friend and leader, Medgar Evers, the civil rights champion, the man with courage. The Klan had sent a thug who shot him when he was coming home one evening. The perpetrator was walking around free, but the movement lay dead with its leader.

And the whites? "Aren't there any white people who are helping you?"

"Oh, some high school kids, but it's dangerous for them. Their father loses his job and the boy gets teased at school, A 'white nigger' is more hated than we are."

Slowly but surely it dawned on me that Charles was turning me into a black man. Gradually I felt my innocence and unquestioned sense of freedom disappear. This country is your enemy. You're riding in a car with a black man, your license plate betrays you as a Freedom Rider on your way to Selma. "They hate the guts out of you." And the fear began to take shape deep in my heart. At first I dismissed it with "It won't get that bad," but it anchored itself deeper and deeper within me. The fear gave me new eyes, new ears, and a new mouth.

"Look, a state trooper, slow down your car....Did you hear what that guy said? He called you a nigger....You belong with us and that's all there is to it....You've made a decision and you've got to suffer the consequences."

ROAD TO PEACE

Thirsty and Out of Gas

After riding through the night for eight hours you get thirsty. There were restaurants along the way where coffee was being served, but not for us. Charles knew it. "We can't stop anywhere. Otherwise we'll end up in jail before we get to Selma." But I was thirsty, and I told him he was exaggerating. One look through the window was enough for me to realize that he was right. A woman saw us coming and quickly shoved a sign into her shop window: "Whites only."

"Do you have enough gas? I hope we can make it to Selma." It's too dangerous to stop at a gas station. They hate us.

On Tuesday morning at six o'clock, tired, dirty, and unshaven, we drove into Selma.

ROAD TO PEACE

Praying Is Never Antisocial

Praying can never be antisocial or asocial. Whenever we pray and leave out our neighbors, our prayer is not real prayer. True prayer by its nature is socially significant.

Compassion means to build a bridge to others without knowing whether they want to be reached.

Compassion is not covered by the word "pity," nor by the word "sympathy." Pity connotes too much distance. Sympathy implies an exclusive nearness. Compassion goes beyond distance and exclusiveness.

Conversion to God…means a simultaneous conversion to the other persons who live with you on this earth. The farmer, the worker, the student, the prisoner, the sick, the black person, the white person, the weak,

51

the strong, the oppressed and the oppressor, the patient and the one who heals, the tortured and the torturer, not only are they people like you, but they are also called to recognize with you that God is a God for all people.

WITH OPEN HANDS

Their Flesh Is My Flesh

Across all barriers of land and language, wealth and poverty, knowledge and ignorance, we are one, created from the same dust, subject to the same laws and destined for the same end. With this compassion you can say, "In the face of the oppressed I recognize my own face and in the hands of the oppressor I recognize my own hands. Their flesh is my flesh; their blood is my blood; their pain is my pain; their smile is my smile. Their ability to torture is in me, too; their capacity to forgive I find also in myself: There is nothing in me that does not belong to them, too. There is nothing in them that does not belong to me, too.

"In my heart, I know their yearning for love, and down to my entrails I can feel their cruelty. In another's eyes, I see my plea for forgiveness, and in a hardened frown, I see my refusal. When someone murders, I know that I too could have done that, and when someone gives birth, I know that I am capable of that as well. In the depths of my being, I meet my fellow humans with whom I share love and hate, life and death."

Compassion is daring to acknowledge our mutual destiny so that we might move forward, all together, into the land which God is showing us.

WITH OPEN HANDS

Love of Power and the Power of Love

What makes the temptation of power so seemingly irresistible? Maybe it is that power offers an easy substitute for the hard task of love. It seems easier to be God than to love God, easier to control people than to love people, easier to own life than to love life.

Jesus asks, "Do you love me?" We ask, "Can we sit at your right hand and your left hand in your Kingdom?" (Mt 20–21). Ever since the snake said, "The day you eat of this tree your eyes will be open and you will be like gods, knowing good from evil" (Gen 3:5), we have been tempted to replace love with power. Jesus lived that temptation in the most agonizing way from the desert to the cross. The long painful history of the Church is the history of people ever and again tempted to choose power over love, control over the cross, being a leader over being led. Those who resisted this temptation to the end and thereby give us hope are the true saints.

IN THE NAME OF JESUS

To Pray Is to Become

*O*ften I have said to people, "I will pray for you," but how often did I really enter into the full reality of what that means? When I really bring my friends and the many I pray for into my innermost being and feel their pains, their struggles, their cries in my own soul, then I leave myself, so to speak, and become them, then I have compassion.

Compassion lies at the heart of our prayer for our fellow human beings. When I pray for the world, I become the world; when I pray for the endless needs of the millions, my soul expands and wants to embrace them all and bring them into the presence of God. But in the midst of that experience I realize that compassion is not mine but God's gift to me. I cannot embrace the world, but God can. I cannot pray, but God can pray in me. When God became as we are, that is, when God allowed all of us to enter into the intimacy of the divine life, it became possible for us to share in God's infinite compassion.

In praying for others I lose myself and become the other, only to be found by the divine love which holds the whole of humanity in a compassionate embrace.

GENESEE DIARY

Real Solitude:
Unlimited Space for Others

There is a powerful connection between poverty and intercessory prayer. When we give up what sets us apart from others—not just property but also opinions, prejudices, judgments, and mental preoccupations—then we can allow friends as well as enemies to enter with us into our solitude and lift them up to God in the midst of the great encounter. In real solitude there is an unlimited space for others, because there we are empty and there we can see that, in fact, nobody stands over and against us. An enemy is only our enemy as long as we have something to defend. But when we have nothing to hold onto, nothing to protect, nothing to consider as exclusively ours, then nobody can be an enemy and then we can, in fact, recognize in the center of our solitude that all men and women are brothers and sisters.

CLOWNING IN ROME

CHRIST IN THE POOR

God Is As Close
As the Poorest Person

Today's readings complement each other in a remarkable way. In the first reading, Moses says, "You shall not steal; …you shall not defraud….You shall not revile the deaf. You shall not render an unjust judgment…. You shall not hate in your heart," and so on (Lev 19:11–17). The *nots* sound harsh and forbidding, like gunshots. But in the second reading, Jesus says, "I was hungry and you gave me food, I was thirsty and you gave me something to drink, I was a stranger and you welcomed me. …Just as you did it to one of the least of these brothers and sisters of mine, you did it to me" (Mt 25:35, 40).

This is the great movement from "you shall not" to "you may." We may care for the poor, the sick, and the dying, and meet God there. Instead of a distant God, whom we must please by not doing evil things, Jesus reveals to us a God who is as close to us as the poorest person is.

I keep marveling at the radicality as well as the simplicity of Jesus' message. He breaks right through all the questions about what to do in order not to offend

God and places the poor in front of us, saying, "This is me
. . . love me." How radical and how simple!

SABBATICAL JOURNEY

People in Need: Wanting to Help

I want to help. I want to do something for people in
need. I want to offer consolation to those who are in grief
and alleviate the suffering of those who are in pain. There
is obviously nothing wrong with that desire. It is a noble
and grace-filled desire. But unless I realize that God's
blessing is coming to me from those I want to serve, my
help will be short-lived, and soon I will be "burned out."

HERE AND NOW

Blessings From the Poor

*H*ow is it possible to keep caring for the poor when
the poor only get poorer? How is it possible to keep
nursing the sick when they are not getting better? How
can I keep consoling the dying when their deaths only
bring me more grief? The answer is that they all hold a
blessing for me, a blessing that I need to receive. Ministry
is, first of all, receiving God's blessing from those to
whom we minister. What is this blessing? It is a glimpse of
the face of God. Seeing God is what heaven is all about!
We can see God in the face of Jesus, and we can see the
face of Jesus in all those who need our care.

HERE AND NOW

Key to the Kingdom

Jean Vanier, the Canadian who founded a worldwide network of communities for mentally disabled people, has remarked more than once that Jesus did not say: "Blessed are those who care for the poor," but "Blessed are the poor." Simple as this remark may seem, it offers the key to the kingdom.

Once I asked Jean Vanier: "How do you find the strength to see so many people each day and listen to their many problems and pains?" He gently smiled and said: "They show me Jesus and give me life." Here lies the great mystery of Christian service. Those who serve Jesus in the poor will be fed by him whom they serve: "He will put on an apron, set them down at table and wait on them" (Lk 12:37).

HERE AND NOW

Become Like Jesus

How does the Spirit of God manifest itself through us? Often we think that to witness means to speak up in defense of God. This idea can make us very self-conscious. We wonder where and how we can make God the topic of our conversations and how to convince our families, friends, neighbors, and colleagues of God's presence in their lives. But this explicit missionary endeavor often comes from an insecure heart and, therefore, easily creates divisions.

The way God's Spirit manifests itself most convincingly is through its fruit: "love, joy, peace, patience, kindness, goodness, trustfulness, gentleness and self-control" (Gal 5:22). These fruits speak for themselves. It is, therefore, always better to raise the question "How can I grow in the Spirit?" than the question "How can I make *others* believe in the Spirit?"

BREAD FOR THE JOURNEY

Going to the Margins of the Church

Those who are marginal in the world are central in the Church, and that is how it is supposed to be! Thus we are called as members of the Church to keep going to the margins of our society. The homeless, the starving, parentless children, people with AIDS, our emotionally disturbed brothers and sisters—they require our first attention.

We can trust that when we reach out with all our energy to the margins of our society we will discover that petty disagreements, fruitless debates, and paralyzing rivalries will recede and gradually vanish. The Church will always be renewed when our attention shifts from ourselves to those who need our care. The blessing of Jesus always comes to us through the poor. The most remarkable experience of those who work with the poor is that, in the end, the poor give more than they receive. They give food to us.

BREAD FOR THE JOURNEY

Who Are the Poor?

The poor are the center of the Church. But who are the poor? At first we might think of people who are not like us: people who live in slums, people who go to soup kitchens, people who sleep on the streets, people in prisons, mental hospitals, and nursing homes. But the poor can be very close. They can be in our own families, churches, or workplaces. Even closer, the poor can be ourselves, who feel unloved, rejected, ignored, or abused.

It is precisely when we see and experience poverty—whether far away, close by, or in our own hearts—that we need to become the Church; that is, hold hands as brothers and sisters, confess our own brokenness and need, forgive one another, heal one another's wounds, and gather around the table of Jesus for the breaking of the bread. Thus, as the poor we recognize Jesus, who became poor for us.

BREAD FOR THE JOURNEY

IV
ᴛURNING POINT

The farther I run away
from the place where God dwells,
the less I am able to hear the voice
that calls me the Beloved,
and the less I hear that voice,
the more entangled I become
in the manipulations and the
power games of the world.

<small>Tʜᴇ Rᴇᴛᴜʀɴ ᴏꜰ ᴛʜᴇ Pʀᴏᴅɪɢᴀʟ Sᴏɴ</small>

Homelessness

Home: An Evocative Symbol

Probably no word better summarizes the suffering of our time than the word "homeless." It reveals one of our deepest and most painful conditions, the condition of not having a sense of belonging, of not having a place where we can feel safe, cared for, protected, and loved.

The first and most obvious quality of a home is its intimacy. When we say: "I do not feel at home here" we express an uneasiness that does not permit intimacy. When we say: "I wish I were home" we express a longing for that intimate place that offers us a sense of belonging. Even though many people suffer much from conflicts at home, even though much emotional suffering finds its roots at home, and even though "broken homes" are increasingly blamed for crimes and illnesses, the word "home" continues to carry with it a warm love and remains one of the most evocative symbols for happiness. The Christian faith even calls us to experience life as "going home" and death as "coming home at last." In Rembrandt's painting of the Prodigal Son, we can see a moving expression of that faith. The loving embrace in

which the old father holds his exhausted son affirms our
deepest desires for a lasting, intimate home.

LIFESIGNS

Leaving Home

Leaving home is much more than a historical event
bound to time and place. It is a denial of the spiritual
reality that I belong to God with every part of my being,
that God holds me safe in an eternal embrace, that I am
indeed carved in the palms of God's hands…. Leaving
home means ignoring the truth that God has "fashioned
me in secret, molded me in the depths of the earth and
knitted me together in my mother's womb." Leaving
home is living as though I do not yet have a home and
must look far and wide to find one.

Home is the center of my being where I can hear the
voice that says: "You are my Beloved, on you my favor
rests"—the same voice that gave life to the first Adam
and spoke to Jesus, the second Adam; the same voice that
speaks to all the children of God and sets them free to
live in a dark world while remaining in the light.

THE RETURN OF THE PRODIGAL SON

God's Dwelling Place

Words for "home" are often used in the Old and New
Testaments. The Psalms are filled with a yearning to dwell
in the house of God, to take refuge under God's wings, and

to find protection in God's holy temple; they praise God's holy place, God's wonderful tent, God's firm refuge. We might even say that "to dwell in God's house" summarizes all the aspirations expressed in these inspired prayers. It is therefore highly significant that Saint John describes Jesus as the Word of God pitching his tent among us (Jn 1:14). He not only tells us that Jesus invites him and his brother Andrew to stay in his home (Jn 1:38–39), but he also shows how Jesus gradually reveals that he himself is the new temple (Jn 2:19) and the new refuge (Mt 11:28). This is most fully expressed in the farewell address, where Jesus reveals himself as the new home: "Make your home in me, as I make mine in you" (Jn 15:4).

The Incarnation: Bringing God Closer

Jesus in whom the fullness of God dwells has become our home. By making his home in us he allows us to make our home in him. By entering into the intimacy of our innermost self he offers us the opportunity to enter into his own intimacy with God. By choosing us as *his* preferred dwelling place he invites us to choose him as *our* preferred dwelling place. This is the mystery of the incarnation. It is beautifully expressed during the Eucharist when the priest pours a little water into the wine, saying: "By the mingling of this water and wine may we come to share in the divinity of him who humbled himself to share in our humanity." God's immeasurable love for us is expressed in this holy interchange. God so much desired to fulfill our deepest yearning for a home that God decided to build a home in us. Thus we can remain fully human and still have our home in God. In this new home the distinction between distance and closeness no longer exists. God, who is furthest away, came closest, by taking on our mortal humanity. Thus God overcomes all distinctions between "distant" and "close" and offers us an intimacy in which we can be most ourselves when most like God.

LIFESIGNS

Home Is As Close As Your Heart

To those who...desperately look for the house of love where they can find the intimacy their hearts desire, Jesus says: "You have a home . . . I am your home . . . claim me as your home . . . you will find it to be the intimate place where I have found my home . . . it is right where you are . . . in your innermost being . . . in your heart." The more attentive we are to such words the more we realize that we do not have to go far to find what we are searching for. The tragedy is that we are so possessed by fear that we do not trust our innermost self as an intimate place but anxiously wander around hoping to find it where we are not. We try to find that intimate place in knowledge, competence, notoriety, success, friends, sensations, pleasure, dreams, or artificially induced states of consciousness. Thus we become strangers to ourselves, people who have an address but are never home.

LIFESIGNS

A Gradual Process
of Coming Home

*D*iscipline in the spiritual life means…a gradual process of coming home to where we belong and listening there to the voice which desires our attention. It is the voice of the "first love." Saint John writes: "We are to love…because God loved us first" (1 Jn 4:19). It is this first love which offers us the intimate place where we can dwell in safety. The first love says: "You are loved long before other people can love you or you can love others. You are accepted long before you can accept others or receive their acceptance. You are safe long before you can offer or receive safety." Home is the place where that first love dwells and speaks gently to us. It requires discipline to come home and listen, especially when our fears are so noisy that they keep driving us outside of ourselves. But when we grasp the truth that we already have a home, we may at last have the strength to unmask the illusions created by our fears and continue to return again and again and again.

Conversion, then, means coming home, and prayer is seeking our home where the Lord has built a home—in the intimacy of our own hearts. Prayer is the most concrete way to make our home in God.

LIFESIGNS

THE RETURN OF THE PRODIGAL SON

A Sense of Homelessness

In the months following the celebration of the thirtieth anniversary of my ordination to the priesthood, I gradually entered into very dark interior places and began to experience immense inner anguish. I came to a point where I could no longer feel safe in my own community and had to leave to seek help in my struggle and to work directly on my inner healing. The few books I could take with me were all about Rembrandt and the parable of the prodigal son. While living in a rather isolated place, far away from my friends and community, I found great consolation in reading the tormented life of the great Dutch painter and learning more about the agonizing journey that ultimately had enabled him to paint this magnificent work.

For hours I looked at the splendid drawings and paintings he created in the midst of all his setbacks, disillusionment, and grief, and I came to understand how from his brush there emerged the figure of a nearly blind old man holding his son in a gesture of all-forgiving compassion.

One must have died many deaths and cried many tears to have painted a portrait of God in such humility.

THE RETURN OF THE PRODIGAL SON

A Love That Always Welcomes Home

The parable of the prodigal son is a story that speaks about a love that existed before any rejection was possible and that will still be there after all rejections have taken place. It is the first and everlasting love of a God who is Father as well as Mother. It is the fountain of all true human love, even the most limited. Jesus' whole life and preaching had only one aim: to reveal this inexhaustible, unlimited motherly and fatherly love of his God and to show the way to let that love guide every part of our daily lives. In his painting of the father, Rembrandt offers me a glimpse of that love. It is the love that always welcomes home and always wants to celebrate.

THE RETURN OF THE PRODIGAL SON

The Younger Son

The younger son's return takes place in the very moment that he reclaims his sonship, even though he has lost all the dignity that belongs to it. In fact, it was the loss of everything that brought him to the bottom line of his identity. He hit the bedrock of his sonship. In retrospect, it seems that the prodigal had to lose everything to come into touch with the ground of his being. When he found himself desiring to be treated as one of the pigs, he realized that he was not a pig but a human being, a son of his father. This realization became the basis for his choice to live instead of to die. Once he had come again in touch with the truth of his sonship, he could hear—although faintly— the voice calling him the Beloved and feel—although distantly—the touch of blessing. This awareness of and confidence in his father's love, misty as it may have been, gave him the strength to claim for himself his sonship, even though that claim could not be based on any merit.

THE RETURN OF THE PRODIGAL SON

The Elder Brother

The elder brother compares himself with the younger one and becomes jealous. But the father loves them both so much that it didn't even occur to him to delay the party in order to prevent the elder son from feeling rejected. I am convinced that many of my emotional problems would melt as snow in the sun if I could let the truth of God's motherly non-comparing love permeate my heart.

How hard that is becomes clear when I reflect on the parable of the laborers in the vineyard. Each time I read that parable in which the landowner gives as much to the workers who worked only one hour as to those who did "a heavy day's work in all the heat," a feeling of irritation still wells up inside of me.

THE RETURN OF THE PRODIGAL SON

Equal Pay for Unequal Work

Why didn't the landowner pay those who worked many long hours first and then surprise the latecomers with his generosity? Why, instead, does he pay the workers of the eleventh hour first, raising false expectations in the others and creating unnecessary bitterness and jealousy? These questions, I now realize, come from a perspective that is all too willing to impose the economy of the temporal on the unique order of the divine.

It hadn't previously occurred to me that the landowner might have wanted the workers of the early hours to rejoice in his generosity to the latecomers. It never crossed my mind that he might have acted on the supposition that those who had worked in the vineyard the whole day would be deeply grateful to have had the opportunity to do work for their boss, and even more grateful to see what a generous man he is. It requires an interior about-face to accept such a non-comparing way of thinking. But that is God's way of thinking. God looks at his people as children of a family who are happy that those who have done only a little bit are as much loved as those who accomplish much.

THE RETURN OF THE PRODIGAL SON

Is God Naive?

God is so naive as to think that there would be great rejoicing when all those who spent time in his vineyard, whether a short time or a long time, were given the same attention. Indeed, he was so naive as to expect that they would all be so happy to be in his presence that comparing themselves with each other wouldn't even occur to them. That is why he says with the bewilderment of a misunderstood lover: "Why should you be envious because I am generous?" He could have said: "You have been with me the whole day, and I gave you all you asked for! Why are you so bitter?" It is the same bewilderment that comes from the heart of the father when he says to his jealous son: "My son, you are with me always, and all I have is yours."

Here lies hidden the great call to conversion: to look not with the eyes of my own low self-esteem, but with the eyes of God's love. As long as I keep looking at God as a landowner, as a father who wants to get the most out of me for the least cost, I cannot but become jealous, bitter, and resentful toward my fellow workers or my brothers and sisters. But if I am able to look at the world with the eyes of God's love and discover that God's vision is not that of a stereotypical landowner or patriarch but rather that of an all-giving and forgiving father who does not measure out his love to his children according to how well they behave, then I quickly see that my only true response can be deep gratitude.

THE RETURN OF THE PRODIGAL SON

71

The Discipline of Gratitude

Gratitude is not a simple emotion or an obvious attitude. It is a difficult discipline to constantly reclaim my whole past as the concrete way in which God has led me to this moment and is sending me into the future. It is hard precisely because it challenges me to face the painful moments—experiences of rejection and abandonment, feelings of loss and failure—and gradually to discover in them the pruning hands of God purifying my heart for deeper love, stronger hope, and broader faith. Jesus says to his disciples that although they are as intimately related to him as branches are to the vine, they still need to be pruned in order to bear more fruit (Jn 15:1–5). Pruning means cutting, reshaping, removing what diminishes vitality. When we look at a pruned vineyard, we can hardly believe it will bear fruit. But when harvesttime comes we realize that the pruning enabled the vine to concentrate its energy and produce more grapes than it could have had it remained unpruned. Grateful people are those who can celebrate even the pains of life because they trust that when harvesttime comes the fruit will show that the pruning was not punishment but purification.

I am gradually learning that the call to gratitude asks us to say "everything is grace."

WEAVINGS

Fear of God Paralyzes

From the beginning I was prepared to accept that not only the younger son, but also the elder son would reveal to me an important aspect of my spiritual journey. For a long time the father remained "the other," the one who would receive me, forgive me, offer me a home, and give me peace and joy. The father was the place to return to, the goal of my journey, the final resting place. It was only gradually and often quite painfully that I came to realize that my spiritual journey would never be complete as long as the father remained an outsider.

It dawned on me that even my best theological and spiritual formation had not been able to completely free me from a Father God who remained somewhat threatening and somewhat fearsome. All I had learned about the Father's love had not fully enabled me to let go of an authority above me who had power over me and would use it according to his will. Somehow, God's love for me was limited by my fear of God's power, and it seemed wise to keep a careful distance even though the desire for closeness was immense. I know that I share this experience with countless others. I have seen how the fear of becoming subject to God's revenge and punishment has paralyzed the mental and emotional lives of many people, independently of their age, religion, or lifestyle. This paralyzing fear of God is one of the great human tragedies.

THE RETURN OF THE PRODIGAL SON

Claiming Spiritual Fatherhood

*B*ut what of the father? Why pay so much attention to the sons when it is the father who is in the center and when it is the father with whom I am to identify? Why talk so much about being like the sons when the real question is: Are you interested in being like the father? It feels somehow good to be able to say: "These sons are like me." It gives a sense of being understood. But how does it feel to say: "The father is like me"? Do I want to be like the father? Do I want to be not just the one who is being forgiven, but also the one who forgives; not just the one who is being welcomed home, but also the one who welcomes home; not just the one who receives compassion, but the one who offers it as well?

Isn't there a subtle pressure in both the Church and society to remain a dependent child? Hasn't the Church in the past stressed obedience in a fashion that made it hard to claim spiritual fatherhood, and hasn't our consumer society encouraged us to indulge in childish self-gratification? Who has truly challenged us to liberate ourselves from immature dependencies and to accept the burden of responsible adults? And aren't we ourselves constantly trying to escape the fearful task of fatherhood? Rembrandt certainly did. Only after much pain and suffering, when he approached death, was he able to understand and paint true spiritual paternity.

THE RETURN OF THE PRODIGAL SON

Returning:
Only a Step on the Way

A child does not remain a child. A child becomes an adult. An adult becomes father and mother. When the prodigal son returns home, he returns not to remain a child, but to claim his sonship and become a father himself. As the returned child of God who is invited to resume my place in my Father's home, the challenge now, yes the call, is to become the Father myself. I am awed by this call. For a long time I have lived with the insight that returning to my Father's home was the ultimate call. It has taken me much spiritual work to make the elder son as well as the younger son in me turn around and receive the welcoming love of the Father. The fact is that, on many levels, I am still returning. But the closer I come to home the clearer becomes the realization that there is a call beyond the call to return. It is the call to become the Father who welcomes home and calls for a celebration. Having reclaimed my sonship, I now have to claim fatherhood. When I first saw Rembrandt's *Prodigal Son*, I could never have dreamt that becoming the repentant son was only a step on the way to becoming the welcoming father. I now see that the hands that forgive, console, heal, and offer a festive meal must become my own.

THE RETURN OF THE PRODIGAL SON

No Soft Interpretation

This call to become the Father precludes any "soft" interpretation of the story. I know how much I long to return and be held safe, but do I really want to be son and heir with all that that implies? Being in the Father's house requires that I make the Father's life my own and become transformed in his image.

As the years of my life pass, I discover how arduous and challenging, but also how fulfilling it is to grow into this spiritual fatherhood. Rembrandt's painting rules out any thought that this has anything to do with power, influence, or control. I might once have held the illusion that one day the many bosses would be gone and I could finally be the boss myself. But this is the way of the world in which power is the main concern. And it is not difficult to see that those who have tried most of their lives to get rid of their bosses are not going to be very different from their predecessors when they finally step into their places. Spiritual fatherhood has nothing to do with power or control. It is a fatherhood of compassion. And I have to keep looking at the Father embracing the prodigal son to catch a glimpse of this.

THE RETURN OF THE PRODIGAL SON

From Forgiven to Forgiver

$\mathcal{P}$erhaps the most radical statement Jesus ever made is: "Be compassionate as your Father is compassionate." God's compassion is described by Jesus not simply to show me how willing God is to feel for me, or to forgive me my sins and offer me new life and happiness, but to invite me to become like God and to show the same compassion to others as he is showing to me. If the only meaning of the story were that people sin but God forgives, I could easily begin to think of my sins as a fine occasion for God to show me his forgiveness. There would be no real challenge in such an interpretation. I would resign myself to my weaknesses and keep hoping that eventually God would close God's eyes to them and let me come home, whatever I did. Such sentimental romanticism is not the message of the Gospels.

What I am called to make true is that whether I am the younger or the elder son, I am the son of my compassionate Father. I am an heir. No one says it more clearly than Paul when he writes: "The Spirit himself joins with our spirit to bear witness that we are children of God. And if we are children, then we are heirs, heirs of God and joint heirs with Christ, provided that we share his sufferings, so as to share his glory." Indeed, as son and heir I am to become successor. I am destined to step into my Father's place and offer to others the same compassion that he has offered me. The return to the Father is ultimately the challenge to become the Father.

THE RETURN OF THE PRODIGAL SON

A HANDBOOK FOR ASPIRING PRODIGALS

In the simplest of terms, the writings of Henri Nouwen may be seen as the record of one human being's struggle to reach spiritual maturity. It is a struggle which engages each and every one of us in recurring cycles throughout our lives. Adolescents must make the hard choices between the tumultuous demands of their hormonal energies and the "thou shalt nots" of their elders. Newlyweds must adjust to the shared life of mutual deferral in contrast to the untethered life of independence and the pursuit of personal goals. Workers must adjust to co-workers and conditions not of their choosing in the workplace. The elderly must learn to cope with failing health, with savings eroded by the spiraling costs of medical care and the escalating cost of everything.

Life has a way of moving us from familiar and comfortable places to new places where we may experience ourselves suddenly as strangers and aliens. From happy homes to broken homes, from finding the perfect mate or perfect friend to the trauma of estrangement or divorce, from the safety and security of belonging to an "in" group to finding ourselves outsiders, because of some disagreement or change in direction. Any one of these experiences might well be described as forms of "homelessness."

In the context of the story of The Return of the Prodigal Son, *it might be said, that of all the forms of separation just mentioned, one of the saddest and most painful in our contemporary world are the separations that can take place within religious groups, and in particular, among Christian communities. In the secular and political realm we expect division and even deviousness. In religious communities that preach love, acceptance, equality, and forgiveness, we expect more. It's the wounds we suffer from religious people and religious institutions that hurt the most. It is within this arena that our struggle toward spiritual maturity can be put to the severest of tests. Nowhere can "homelessness" be felt more deeply than when we feel estranged from the Christian community.*

Nouwen's writings show clearly that he experienced many of the human struggles with which we all have to deal. His writings invite us to identify with him and to learn from him as we deal with our own struggle toward maturity, toward personal and communal integration.

Nouwen's book, The Return of the Prodigal Son, *marks a climactic turning point in his own personal search. It is regarded by many as the crowning work of all his writings. It is different in that it marks a departure from the way most of us have become accustomed to interpret the story. It's easy to say of the renegade son: "That's me. I'm the one who has wandered off the beaten path. I'm the ingrate who needs to come back and seek forgiveness." Nouwen, while identifying with the prodigal, as most of us might, moves beyond that, concluding that the story calls him ultimately to identify with the Father. It's important to point out that he didn't see it this way from the beginning.*

I gained access to how he arrived at that conclusion when I visited him in the spring of 1992, at the time when the first copies of the book arrived at his office. His community was in a celebrative mood, seeing the book he had worked on with such dedication, hot off the press in a beautifully bound hardcover edition. I was in the kitchen talking to Elizabeth, a member of the Daybreak community, who was washing dishes. As we were discussing the book, she said to me: "You must understand (referring to Nouwen's identifying with the Father in the parable): he didn't see it that way from the start. He had no problem identifying with the younger son and the elder son, but when it came to the Father, he didn't know what to do. What could he say about the Father except that the Father showed us how good and merciful God is. End of the story."

But those around Nouwen insisted: "YOU ARE THE FATHER. You are the pastor of this community. You minister to us. You are the one who leads and forgives. YOU ARE THE FATHER!" Nouwen recoiled from any such comparison, feeling it would be the height of arrogance to make such a claim. Finally, in exasperation one of the women in the group blurted out: "But the son doesn't stay a son forever! The son has to grow up and become a Father himself!"

That cinched it. Nouwen could not argue the point. There was nothing left to do but yield to impenetrable logic. The rest is in the book. And it leaves none of the rest of us off the hook.

It's nice to identify with the prodigal who gets the royal welcome, the bear hug. It's nice sporting the ring, the best robe, the designer sandals, telling a hard luck story to a captive audience over a sizzling barbecue. But in Nouwen's telling at the urging of his community, this story cuts two ways. As the younger son, we are also called to grow up. And to move beyond being the life of the party to being the life-giver of the party. To move beyond being the forgiven to being the forgiver. In short, we are called to grow to spiritual maturity: to move from being receivers to being givers.

How does one advance to spiritual maturity? Like all growth, usually by passing through succeeding stages, some of them painful. Though published four years later, closely related to Nouwen's book, The Return of the Prodigal Son, is The Inner Voice of Love, a private journal Nouwen kept during a very painful period he passed through in the final months of 1988. He refers briefly to this trial-by-fire in the concluding pages of The Road to Daybreak (p. 222ff), but very explicitly in The Inner Voice of Love (1996). Given its personal nature, the journal was not intended for publication. Nevertheless, with the elapse of time he allowed a few intimate friends to read it. His friends strongly urged publication. After much hesitation he agreed to release it for publication eight years after it was written, but only after extensive editing.

He explains in his Introduction: "This book is my secret journal. It was written during the most difficult period of my life, from December 1987 to June 1988. That was a time of extreme anguish, during which I wondered whether I would be able to hold on to my life. Everything came crashing down, my self-esteem, my energy to live and work, my sense of being loved, my hope for healing, my trust in God…everything."

The book is a collection of what Nouwen calls "spiritual imperatives," sixty-two in all, a rich resource of spiritual wisdom. "Silver bullets," one might call them, aimed to pierce *to the core of the human heart. I have selected three of the imperatives to serve as a bridge to link the themes of "Home-coming" and "Growing to Spiritual Maturity" with the major themes to follow, namely "Spiritual Direction" and "Community." We begin with an appeal to the wandering prodigal: Come Home!*

Come Home

There are two realities to which you must cling. First, God has promised that you will receive the love you have been searching for. And second, God is faithful to that promise.

So stop wandering around. Instead, come home and trust that God will bring you what you need. Your whole life you have been running about, seeking the love you desire. Now it is time to end that search. Trust that God will give you that all-fulfilling love and will give it in a human way. Before you die, God will offer you the deepest satisfaction you can desire. Just stop running and start trusting and receiving.

Home is where you are truly safe. It is where you can receive what you desire. You need human hands to hold you there so you don't run away again. But when you come home and stay home, you will find the love that will bring rest to your heart.

THE INNER VOICE OF LOVE

82

Avoid All Forms
of Self-Rejection

You must avoid not only blaming others but also blaming yourself. You are inclined to blame yourself for the difficulties you experience in relationships. But self-blame is not a form of humility. It is a form of self-rejection in which you ignore or deny your own goodness and beauty.

When a friendship does not blossom, when a word is not received, when a gesture of love is not appreciated, do not blame it on yourself. This is both untrue and hurtful. Every time you reject yourself, you idealize others. You want to be with those whom you consider better, stronger, more intelligent, more gifted than yourself. Thus you make yourself emotionally dependent, leading others to feel unable to fulfill your expectations and causing them to withdraw from you. This makes you blame yourself even more, and you enter a dangerous spiral of self-rejection and neediness.

Avoid all forms of self-rejection. Acknowledge your limitations, but claim your unique gifts and thereby live as an equal among equals. That will set you free from your obsessive and possessive needs and enable you to give and receive true affection and friendship.

THE INNER VOICE OF LOVE

Remain Anchored
in Your Community

It is important to remain as much in touch as possible with those who know you, love you, and protect your vocation. If you visit people with great needs and deep struggles that you can easily recognize in your own heart, remain anchored in your home community. Think about your community as holding a long line that girds your waist. Wherever you are, it holds that line. Thus you can be very close to people in need of your healing without losing touch with those who protect your vocation. Your community can pull you back when its members see that you are forgetting why you were sent out.

When you feel a burgeoning need for sympathy, support, affection, and care from those to whom you are being sent, remember that there is a place where you can receive those gifts in a safe and responsible way. Do not let yourself be seduced by the dark powers that imprison those you want to set free. Keep returning to those to whom you belong and who keep you in the light. It is that light that you desire to bring into the darkness. You do not have to fear anyone as long as you remain safely anchored in your community. Then you can carry the light far and wide.

THE INNER VOICE OF LOVE

If there is one theme evident in the three selections quoted above and throughout the journal from which they are taken, it is the recognition of our need for support of one another in our human journey. If this is true at the level of the give and take of our everyday lives, it is all the more true of our spiritual journey, where the terrain is not clearly staked out with road maps and sign posts every step of the way. Nouwen had to deal with this at a very personal level when he accepted the position offered him in 1971 as associate professor of pastoral theology at Yale Divinity School. Students flocked to his lectures and sought him out in coffee hours and private gatherings outside of class. These were students who, for the greater part were being trained for ministry. They were full of questions about their own spiritual journeys as well as about others they would be expected to lead in the years ahead.

It was out of this situation that Nouwen's writings continued to flow. He would begin preparing a lecture, hold meetings with a few key assistants from the student body to seek their input on the ideas he was hoping to develop, take notes, deliver the lectures, refine his ideas further, and eventually submit a completed work for publication. Well known from this era are his monographs, Wounded Healer, Out of Solitude, Reaching Out, and The Way of the Heart, to mention only a few. Less known is a work he published originally for Yale's house publication, Reflection, entitled "Spiritual Direction" (January 1981). Though it was subsequently published in pamphlet form as well as in Worship magazine (September 1981), it is still not as accessible to the general reader as Nouwen's larger works since the complete piece has not yet appeared in popular book form. Because of its importance from a pastoral point of view and the link it provides to the themes we are exploring in this work, the essay is reproduced here in its entirety.

To reorient ourselves: Once one has followed through on the decision to "come home," a new question soon emerges: Where does one go from there? In the Gospel story, the prodigal son makes his way back, receives an overwhelmingly generous reception, and that's where the story ends. The focus is on the goodness of the Father, not on the ensuing history of the son. For the rest of us, our homecomings aren't usually experienced that dramatically. There may be tears or deeply felt emotions at decisive turning points in our relationship with God or with one another. But when the moment of climax has passed, one is left to build or not build on the grace received. As Nouwen put it, referring to the elder son in the parable: One can be home and lost at home.

Spiritual masters instill into the minds and hearts of their disciples: Not to go forward is to go backward. It is out of this conviction that the discipline of spiritual direction has grown from a long-standing tradition in the history of spirituality. In the essay that follows Nouwen provides a summation of some of the basic elements present in the notion of spiritual direction. Again, a reminder: the text has been selected as a sequel to stimulate reflection on the question raised above: After you've come home, where do you go from there? Nouwen offers a handy guidebook for those who wish to move from being homebodies to being explorers and community builders.

V
COMMITMENT

*Maturation in a spiritual sense is
a growing willingness to stretch out my arms,
to have a belt put around me and
to be led where I would rather not go
(Jn 21:18).*

GRACIAS! A LATIN AMERICAN JOURNAL

SPIRITUAL DIRECTION

Guidance in Our Relationship With God

Spiritual direction is direction given to people in their relationship with God. Just as a creative dialogue with other human beings cannot just be left to our natural responses, so too our intimate conversation with God needs formation and training. Precisely the fact that we are dealing here with the most intimate and precious relationship is the reason for direction. It is therefore not so strange that people who search for a deep and persistent prayer life always ask for some help. During the past decade more and more people have been looking for some kind of guidance in their relationship with God and are appealing to their ministers to offer such guidance. In these reflections, I would like to offer a few ideas which might help in defining the nature of this ministry of spiritual direction and which might begin to suggest some concrete ways in which this ministry can be practiced.

SPIRITUAL DIRECTION

Movement From
Absurdity to Obedience

The spiritual life is a life in which we struggle to
move from absurd living to obedient living. The word
absurd includes the word *surdus* which means "deaf."
Absurd living is a way of life in which we remain deaf to
the voice which speaks to us in our silence. The many
activities in which we are involved, the many concerns
which keep us preoccupied and the many sounds which
surround us, make it very hard for us to hear the small
voice through which God makes God's presence known
(see 1 Kgs 19:12). It seems that the world in which we
live conspires against our hearing that voice and tries to
make us absolutely deaf. It therefore is not surprising that
we often wonder, in the midst of our very occupied and
preoccupied lives, if anything is truly happening. Our
lives might be filled with many events—so many events
even that we often wonder how we can get it all done—
but at the same time we might feel very unfulfilled, and
wonder if anything is happening which is worth living for.
Being filled yet unfulfilled, being busy yet bored, being
involved yet lonely, these are symptoms of the absurd life,
the life in which we are no longer hearing the voice of
the One who created us and who keeps calling us to a
new life in God. This absurd life is extremely painful,
because it makes us feel as if we are living in exile, cut off
from the vital source of our existence.

SPIRITUAL DIRECTION

Listening to the Voice of God

The obedient life forms the other end of the spiritual spectrum. The word *obedience* includes the word *audire* which means "listening." Living a spiritually mature life is living a life in which we listen to the voice of God's Spirit within and among us and in which we try to respond to that voice at every moment of our lives. The great news of God's revelation is not simply that God exists but also that God is actively present in our lives at all times and at all places. Our God is a God who cares, heals, guides, directs, challenges, confronts, corrects. God is a God who wants to lead us closer to the full realization of our humanity. To be obedient means to be constantly attentive to this active presence of God and to allow God, who is only love, to be the source as well as the goal of all we think, say, and do. It is, however, far from easy to live a life of listening. There are strong resistances in us to listening.

SPIRITUAL DIRECTION

Creating an Empty Space

First of all, we find it very hard to create some empty space in our lives and to give up our occupations and preoccupations, even for a while. We suffer from a fear of the empty space. We are so concerned to be useful, effective, and in control, that a useless, ineffective, and uncontrollable moment scares us and drives us right back to the security of having something valuable to do. But even stronger than our fear of the empty space is our fear of the voice of God which we might come to hear there. We know that our God is a jealous God and God's mercy is a severe mercy. And although we are unsatisfied and unfulfilled, we are not so sure that we want to go into the direction God might call us to go. Those who have really listened to God's voice have often found themselves being called away from familiar and relatively comfortable places to places they would rather not go. This was true for the Israelites who complained to Moses that the unpleasant certainty of Egypt seemed preferable to the unpredictable wandering in the desert, and this was even more true for the many men and women who followed Christ and found themselves subject to persecution and painful trials.

SPIRITUAL DIRECTION

A Willingness to Stretch Out Your Hands

Thus the movement from absurdity to obedience is far from easy. It asks for discipline. Discipline in the spiritual life is the other side of discipleship. To follow Christ in the way of the cross requires not the human effort to put on your own belt and walk where you like, but the generous willingness to stretch out your hands and to let somebody else put a belt around you and take you where you would rather not go (see Jn 21:18).

SPIRITUAL DIRECTION

Three Disciplines of the Spiritual Life

In order to overcome our strong resistances to listening and become truly obedient people we need disciplines. The three disciplines which can help us continually to move away from absurd living to obedient living are the discipline of the Church, the discipline of the Book, and the discipline of the heart. These three disciplines can show us clearly what spiritual direction means since they all three are connected with the art of becoming listeners to God's voice.

SPIRITUAL DIRECTION

The Discipline of the Church

The first and most important discipline by which we can become true listeners is the discipline of the Church. The Church is the people of God witnessing to the active presence of God in history. The Church reminds us continuously of what really is happening. In the year-round liturgy the Church unfolds for us the fullness of the Christ-event. Christ is coming, Christ is being born, Christ manifests himself to the world, Christ is suffering, Christ is dying, Christ is being raised up, Christ is ascending into heaven, Christ is sending the Spirit. These events are not simply events which took place long ago and which are remembered with a certain melancholy, but they are events which take place in the day to day life of the Christian community. There is a true answer to the question: "Is anything happening?" In and through the Christ-event, God is making his active presence known to us. That is what Advent, Christmas, Epiphany, Lent, Easter, Ascension, and Pentecost are all about. The Church asks our attention to the divine events which underlie all of history and which allow us to make sense out of our own story. Thus the Church directs our listening. The more we let the Christ-event inform and form us, the more we will be able to connect our own daily stories with the great story of God's presence in our lives. Thus the Church is our first spiritual director by directing our hearts and minds to God, who makes our lives truly eventful.

SPIRITUAL DIRECTION

The Discipline of the Book

The second discipline is the discipline of the Book. When we are really committed to moving away from an absurd life towards an obedient life, we have to keep listening in a very personal and intimate way to the Word of God as it comes to us through the scriptures. The discipline of the Book is the discipline of meditation. Meditation means to let the Word descend from our minds into our hearts and thus to become flesh in us. Meditation means eating the word, digesting it and incorporating it concretely into our lives. Meditation is the discipline by which we let the Word of God become a word for us and anchor itself in the center of our being. In this way, meditation is the ongoing incarnation of God in our world.

While the discipline of the Church keeps reminding us of what is really happening, the discipline of the Book leads us on the road to true inner obedience. Through the regular practice of scriptural meditation we develop an inner ear that allows us to recognize God's Word as a word that speaks directly to our most intimate needs and aspirations. When we listen to a sentence, a story, or a parable not simply to be instructed, informed, or inspired but to be formed into a truly obedient person the Book becomes a spiritual director to us.

SPIRITUAL DIRECTION

The Discipline of the Heart

*F*inally, there is the discipline of the heart. This discipline makes us aware that praying is not only listening *to* but also listening *with*. The discipline of the heart makes us stand in the presence of God with all we have and are: our fears and anxieties, our guilt and shame, our sexual fantasies, our greed and anger, our joys, successes, aspirations and hopes, our reflections, dreams and mental wandering, and most of all our people, family, friends and enemies, in short, all that makes us who we are. With all this we have to listen to God's voice and allow God to speak to us in every corner of our being. This is very hard since we are so fearful and insecure that we keep hiding ourselves from God.

We tend to present to God only those parts of ourselves with which we feel relatively comfortable and which we think will evoke a positive response. Thus our prayer becomes very selective and narrow. And not just our prayers but also our self-knowledge, because by behaving as strangers before God we become strangers to ourselves.

Spiritual Direction

Submitting to a Spiritual Guide

*I*t is of great value to submit our prayer life from time to time to the supervision of a spiritual guide. A spiritual director in this strict sense is not a counselor, a therapist, or an analyst, but a mature fellow Christian to whom we choose to be accountable for our spiritual life and from whom we can expect prayerful guidance in our constant struggle to discern God's active presence in our lives. A spiritual director can be called "soul-friend" (Kenneth Leech) or a "spiritual friend" (Tilden Edwards). It is important that he or she practice the disciplines of the Church and the Book and thus become familiar with the space in which we try to listen to God's voice.

The way we relate to our spiritual director depends very much on our needs, our personalities, and external circumstances. Some people may want to see their spiritual director bi-weekly or monthly, others will find it sufficient to be in touch only when the occasion asks for it. Some people may feel the need for a more extensive sharing with their spiritual director, while others will find seeing him or her once in a while for a few short moments to be sufficient. It is essential that one Christian helps another Christian to enter without fear into the presence of God and there to discern God's call.

SPIRITUAL DIRECTION

The Church, the Book, and a Soul-Friend

Thus the Church, the Book, and a "Soul-friend" are three spiritual directors capable of helping us to overcome our deafness and become free to hear God's voice even when it calls us to unknown places.

During a period of history in which many traditional ways of living are breaking down and in which we are more than ever thrown back on our own personal resources, the need for spiritual direction is rapidly growing. Many people are asking their religious leaders to help them find their way through the complex labyrinth of contemporary living. They are asking: "How can I remain aware of God's presence in my life?" "How can I have some assurance that my decisions about money, work, and relationships are made in the Spirit of the Gospel?" "How do I know that my life is lived in obedience to God and not just in response to my own impulses and desires?"

For some people these questions become very specific: "Should I live a more simple life?" "Should I change my ways of eating and dressing?" "Should I take a more prophetic stance on issues such as the arms race and world hunger?" "Should I maybe give a few years of my life to work with the poor?" All such questions ask for direction because they all require the ability to listen to God's voice. That is why in the spiritual life the real question is not what we are thinking, saying, or doing, but whether or not our thoughts, words, and actions are an obedient response to God's call.

SPIRITUAL DIRECTION

What Finally Counts

How can this direction be offered? I think that it would be a mistake to think only in terms of individual directors. There simply will not be enough people nor enough time to offer this type of ministry. It is important that we are thinking about a ministry in which we help one another to practice the disciplines of the Church, the Book, and the Heart and thus live a life in which we become more and more sensitive to the ongoing presence of God in our lives. What finally counts is not just that there are good spiritual men and women in this very chaotic world, but that there are communities of Christians who together listen with great care and sensitivity to God who wants to make his healing presence known to all people.

SPIRITUAL DIRECTION

ROLE OF THE COMMUNITY IN SPIRITUAL DIRECTION

It should be noted that Nouwen concludes his teaching on the discipline of spiritual direction by pointing out that in today's world the opportunity of having regular access to an individual director in a one-on-one relationship is not likely to be available to many. In the practical order he bids us to think instead in terms of helping one another in the context of community. This emphasis on community is prominent throughout Nouwen's writings. In the ideal order Nouwen would have us understand the Christian community itself as a primary source of spiritual direction. For this reason he emphasizes the importance of belonging to community, building community, developing ministries within the community, understanding the community as the privileged place divinely ordained to mediate the presence and action of God. It seems appropriate then, that in the following section we should focus on a theme so central to the thought of Henri Nouwen.

Private Prayer Needs Support of Community

Much that has been said about prayer thus far might create the false impression that prayer is a private, individualistic and nearly secret affair, so personal and so deeply hidden in our inner life that it can hardly be talked about, even less be shared. The opposite is true. Just because prayer is so personal and arises from the center of our life, it is to be shared with others. Just because prayer is the most precious expression of being human, it needs the constant support and protection of the community to grow and flower. Just because prayer is our highest vocation needing careful attention and faithful perseverance, we cannot allow it to be a private affair. Just because prayer asks for a patient waiting in expectation, it should never become the most individualistic expression of the most individualistic emotion, but should always remain embedded in the life of the community of which we are part.

REACHING OUT

The Right Question

That God reveals the fullness of divine love first of all in community, and that the proclamation of the good news finds its main source there has radical consequences for our lives. Because now, the question is no longer: *How can I best develop my spiritual life and share it with others?*

but *Where do we find the community of faith to which the Spirit of God descends and from which God's message of hope and love can be brought as a light into the world?* Once this question becomes our main concern we can no longer separate the spiritual life from life in community, belonging to God from belonging to each other and seeing Christ from seeing one another in him.

BEHOLD THE BEAUTY OF THE LORD

Community: A Deep Sense of Being Gathered by God

It is important to keep ourselves from thinking about community only in terms of living together in one house, or sharing meals and prayers, or doing projects together. These might well be true expressions of community, but community is a much deeper reality. People who live together do not necessarily live in community, and those who live alone do not necessarily live without it. Physical nearness or distance is secondary. The primary quality of community is a deep sense of being gathered by God. When Francis Xavier traveled alone across many continents to preach the Gospel, he found strength in the sure knowledge that he belonged to a community that supported him with prayer and brotherly care. And many Christians who show great perseverance in hard and lonely tasks find their strength in the deep bond with the community in whose name they do their work.

Here we touch one of the most critical areas of the

Christian life today. Many very generous Christians find themselves increasingly tired and dispirited not so much because the work is hard or the success slight, but because they feel isolated, unsupported, and left alone. People who say, "I wonder if anyone cares what I am doing. I wonder if my superior, my friends at home, or the people who sent me ever think about me, ever pray for me, ever consider me part of their lives," are in real spiritual danger. We are able to do many hard things, tolerate many conflicts, overcome many obstacles, and persevere under many pressures, but when we no longer experience ourselves as part of a caring, supporting, praying community, we quickly lose faith. This is because faith in God's compassionate presence can never be separated from experiencing God's presence in the community to which we belong.

The crises in the lives of many caring Christians today are closely connected with deep feelings of not belonging. Without a sense of being sent by a caring community, a compassionate life cannot last long and quickly degenerates into a life marked by numbness and anger. This is not simply psychological observation, but a theological truth, because apart from a vital relationship with a caring community a vital relationship with Christ is not possible.

COMPASSION

Basis of Community: The Divine Call

The basis of the Christian community is not the family tie or social or economic equality, or shared oppression or complaint, or mutual attraction . . . but the divine call. The Christian community is not the result of human efforts. God has made us into chosen people by calling us out of "Egypt" to the "New Land," out of the desert to fertile ground, out of slavery to freedom, out of our sin to salvation, out of captivity to liberation. All these words and images give expression to the fact that the initiative belongs to God and that God is the source of our new life together. By our common call to the New Jerusalem, we recognize each other on the road as brothers and sisters. Therefore, as the people of God, we are called *ekklesia* (from the Greek *kaleo* = call; and *ek* = out), the community called out of the old world into the new.

Since our desire to break the chains of our alienation is very strong today, it is of special importance to remind each other that, as members of the Christian community, we are not primarily for each other but for God. Our eyes should not remain fixed on each other but be directed forward to what is dawning on the horizon of our existence. We discover each other by following the same vocation and by supporting each other in the same search. Therefore, the Christian community is not a closed circle of people embracing each other, but a forward-moving group of companions bound together by the same voice asking for their attention.

REACHING OUT

Transcending Individual Differences

It is quite understandable that in our large anonymous cities we look for people on our "'wave length'" to form small communities. Prayer groups, Bible-study clubs and house-churches all are ways of restoring or deepening our awareness of belonging to the people of God. But sometimes a false type of like-mindedness can narrow our sense of community. We all should have the mind of Jesus Christ, but we do not all have to have the mind of a school teacher, a carpenter, a bank director, a congressman or whatever socioeconomic or political group. There is a great wisdom hidden in the old bell tower calling people with very different backgrounds away from their homes to form one body in Jesus Christ. It is precisely by transcending the many individual differences that we can become witnesses of God who allows Divine light to shine upon poor and rich, healthy and sick alike. But it is also in this encounter on the way to God that we become aware of our neighbor's needs and begin to heal each other's wounds.

REACHING OUT

Prayer: The Language of the Community

Prayer is the language of the Christian community. In prayer the nature of the community becomes visible because in prayer we direct ourselves to the one who forms the community. We do not pray to each other, but together we pray to God, who calls us and makes us into a new people. Praying is not one of the many things the community does. Rather, it is its very being. Many discussions about prayer do not take this very seriously. Sometimes it seems as if the Christian community is "so busy" with its projects and plans that there is neither the time nor the mood to pray. But when prayer is no longer its primary concern, and when its many activities are no longer seen and experienced as part of prayer itself, the community quickly degenerates into a club with a common cause but no common vocation.

By prayer, community is created as well as expressed. Prayer is first of all the realization of God's presence in the midst of his people and, therefore, the realization of the community itself. Most clear and most noticeable are the words, the gestures and the silence through which the community is formed. When we listen to the word, we not only receive insight into God's saving work, but we also experience a new mutual bond. When we stand around the altar, eat bread and drink wine, kneel in meditation, or walk in procession we not only remember God's work in human history, but we also become aware of God's creative presence here and now. When we sit together in silent prayer, we create a space where we sense that the One we are waiting for is already touching us, as he touched Elijah standing in front of the cave (1 Kgs 19:13).

Words of Longing

But the same words, gestures, and silence are also the ways in which the community reaches out to the one it is waiting for. The words we use are words of longing. The little piece of bread we eat and the little portion of wine we drink make us aware of our most profound hunger and thirst, and the silence deepens our sensitivity to the calling voice of God. Therefore, the prayer of the community is also the expression of its unfulfillment and desire to reach the house of God. Thus the praying community celebrates God's presence while waiting, and affirms God's absence while recognizing that God is already in its midst. Thus God's presence becomes a sign of hope and God's absence a call for penance.

REACHING OUT

Communal and Individual Prayer As Two Folded Hands

Prayer as the language of the community is like our mother tongue. Just as a child learns to speak from his parents, brothers, sisters, and friends but still develops his own unique way of expressing himself, so also our individual prayer life develops by the care of the praying community. Sometimes it is hard to point to any specific organizational structure which we can call "our community." Our community is often a very intangible reality made up of people, living as well as dead, present as well as absent, close as well as distant, old as well as young. But without some form of community, individual prayer cannot be born or developed. Communal and individual prayer belong together as two folded hands. Without community, individual prayer easily degenerates into egocentric and eccentric behavior, but without individual prayer, the prayer of the community quickly becomes a meaningless routine. Individual and community prayer cannot be separated without harm. This explains why spiritual leaders tend to be very critical of those who want to isolate themselves and why they stress the importance of continuing ties with a larger community where individual prayer can be guided. This also explains why the same leaders have always encouraged the individual members of their communities to spend time and energy in personal prayer, realizing as they do that community alone can never fulfill the desire for the most unique intimate relationship between a human being and his or her God.

REACHING OUT

Together We Reach Out

The prayer of our heart can grow strong and deep within the boundaries of the community of faith. The community of faith, strengthened in love by our individual prayers, can lift them up as a sign of hope in common praise and thanksgiving. Together we reach out to God beyond our many individual limitations while offering each other the space for our own most personal search. We may be very different people with different nationalities, colors, histories, characters, and aspirations, but God has called all of us away from the darkness of our illusions into the light of Divine glory.

REACHING OUT

What Is Community?

Someone once said that "community is the place where the person you least want to live with always lives." I mean there is always that one person.

PARTING WORDS

Community Is Not Sentimental Life

In every community—whether family or congregation there is always someone who for someone else is a hair shirt, but that is essential for community. It may not be that we want it, but it is always there. It is not the sentimental life that we want community to be where everybody loves each other. That's never going to be there. People have to be trained to realize that community doesn't mean emotional, affective, total harmony. That's not even good, for we are always on the way, on the move. Imagine if community were all we want it to be, we'd never want to go anywhere. We are a people on the road.

PARTING WORDS

Table As Barometer

Although the table is a place for intimacy, we all know how easily it can become a place of distance, hostility, and even hatred. Precisely because the table is meant to be an intimate place, it easily becomes the place we experience the absence of intimacy. The table reveals the tensions among us. When husband and wife don't talk to each other, when a child refuses to eat, when brothers and sisters bicker, when there are tense silences, then the table becomes hell, the place we least want to be. The table is the barometer of family and community life.

BREAD FOR THE JOURNEY

Forgiveness Is a Word for Love

Forgiveness means that I continually am willing to forgive the other person for not being God—for not fulfilling all my needs. I, too, must ask forgiveness for not being able to fulfill other people's needs.

Our heart—the center of our being—is a part of God. Thus, our heart longs for satisfaction, for total communion. But human beings…are all so limited in giving that which we crave. Since we want so much and we get only part of what we want, we have to keep on forgiving people for not giving us all we want. So I forgive you since you can only love me in a limited way. I forgive my mother that she is not everything I would like her to be. I forgive my father. This is of enormous importance right now because constantly people look to blame their parents, the church, and their friends for not giving them what they need. So many are so angry. They cannot forgive people for offering only limited expressions of an unlimited love. God's love is unlimited but people's love is not. If you enter into any relationship in communion, friendship, marriage, community, the relationships are always riddled with frustration and disappointments. So forgiveness becomes the word for love in the human context.

PARTING WORDS

Forgiveness: The Way to Freedom

To forgive another person from the heart is an act of liberation. We set that person free from the negative bonds that exist between us. We say, "I no longer hold your offense against you." But there is more. We also free ourselves from the burden of being the "offended one." As long as we do not forgive those who have wounded us, we carry them with us or, worse, pull them as a heavy load. The great temptation is to cling in anger to our enemies and then define ourselves as being offended and wounded by them. Forgiveness, therefore, liberates not only the other but also ourselves. It is the way to the freedom of the children of God.

BREAD FOR THE JOURNEY

COMMITMENT – PART 3

*I*NTIMACY AND SOLIDARITY

In God's House No One Is Excluded

*W*hen we use the word "intimacy" in our daily lives we easily associate it with privacy, smallness, coziness, and a certain exclusiveness. When someone refers to a conversation or a party as intimate we tend to think about a few people, a small space, or confidential subject matter. The word "intimate" usually suggests the opposite of being open to the public.

But here our spiritual experience shows us something quite new. Those who have entered deeply into their hearts and found the intimate home where they encounter their Lord come to the mysterious discovery that solidarity is the other side of intimacy. They come to the awareness that the intimacy of God's house excludes no one and includes everyone. They start to see that the home they have found in their innermost being is as wide as the whole of humanity.

Just as distance and closeness are no longer valid distinctions within God's house, so intimacy and solidarity are no longer valid distinctions either. It is of great importance to see the inner connection between intimacy and solidarity. If we fail to recognize this connection our spirituality will become either privatized or narrowly activist and will no longer reflect the full beauty of living in God's house.

LIFESIGNS

All Humanity Gathered in Christ

The best way to see the interconnectedness of intimacy and solidarity is to recall and enter more deeply into the words of Saint John: "The Word was made flesh and pitched his tent among us" (1:14). These words express the mystery that God, in whom all was created, has become part of that same creation. God, who was rejected by our sins, became sin for us in order to offer us a share in the divine life. Thus, in Jesus Christ all humanity has been gathered and led toward God's house. Through the incarnation of God in Jesus Christ all human flesh has been lifted up into God's own intimacy. There is no human being in the past, present, or future, in East, West, North, or South, who has not been embraced by God in and through the flesh of the Word.

LIFESIGNS

A Christ in Whom All People Are Not Gathered Is Not the True Christ

The life, death, and resurrection of Jesus manifest to us the full intimacy of this divine embrace. He lived our lives, died our deaths, and lifted all of us up into his glory. There is no human suffering that has not been suffered in the agony of Jesus on the cross, no human joy that has not been celebrated by Jesus in his resurrection to new life. There is no human death that Jesus has not died, no human life that Jesus has not lived. In him through whom all has been created, all has been restored to the glory of God.

The mystery of the incarnation reveals to us the spiritual dimension of human solidarity. Because all humanity has been taken up into God through the incarnation of the Word, finding the heart of God means finding all the people of God. Therefore, a Christ in whom all people are not gathered together is not the true Christ. We who belong to Christ belong to all of humanity....

We cannot live in intimate communion with Jesus without being sent to our brothers and sisters who belong to that same humanity that Jesus has accepted as his own. Thus intimacy manifests itself as solidarity and solidarity as intimacy.

LIFESIGNS

Living Fully

Being back in France makes me think much about countries and cultures. During the past few months I have been in Holland, Germany, Canada, the United States, and England, and in all these countries I have had intense contact with people and their ways of living, praying, and playing.

There is a great temptation to want to know which culture is the best and where I am most happy and at home. But this way of thinking leads to endless frustrations because the Dutch, the Germans, the French, the Americans, and the Canadians are all people who have unique ways of feeling, thinking, and behaving, none of which totally fits my needs, but all of which have gifts for me.

I know people who complain about the Germans while in Germany and about the Americans while in America, moving themselves and their families back and forth, always wondering what the best place is to live without ever being truly content. Some people, then, are always disappointed with someone or something. They complain about the rigidity of the German Church and the sloppiness of the American Church. Or they may complain about the critical attitude of the Dutch, the mystical attitude of the French, the pragmatic attitude of the Americans, and the formalistic attitude of the English, while never really worshiping deeply at any one place.

I am increasingly aware of how important it is to enjoy

what is given and to fully live where one is. If I could just fully appreciate the need for independence of the Dutch, the spiritual visions of the French, the concreteness of the Americans, the theological concepts of the Germans, and the sense of ceremony of the English, I could come to learn much about life everywhere and truly become present to where I am, always growing deeper in the spirit of gratitude.

Do we really need to belong to one country or one culture? In our world, where distances are becoming less each day, it seems important to become less and less dependent on one place, one language, one culture, or one style of life, but to experience oneself as a member of the human family, belonging to God and free to be wherever we are called to be. I even wonder if the ability to be in so many places so quickly and so often is not an invitation to grow deeper in the spirit and let our identity be more rooted in God and less in the place in which we happen to be.

THE ROAD TO DAYBREAK

EUCHARIST AND COMMUNITY

Presence of Christ

*D*uring the last ten years I have come to see how the Eucharist can create deep, lasting community among people. For many years I thought that the Eucharist was first of all a celebrative expression of an already existing community. Although this is true, my recent experience has shown me that the Eucharist creates community as well as expresses it.

I started a daily Eucharist at two universities with one or two students. Gradually more came, people who did not know each other, and had very different ideas or viewpoints in religious matters, and were quite different in age, nationality, and lifestyle. Most of these people would never have chosen each other as friends or companions. But they all, often for quite different reasons, felt attracted to a daily Eucharistic celebration, in which the Word of God was proclaimed and the Body and Blood of Christ shared. Over the months these quite different people found themselves drawn by Word and Sacrament into a deep community. They discovered a bond based not on physical or emotional attractiveness, social compatibility or common interests, but on the presence of the living Christ among them. Confessing their sins together, accepting together God's mercy, listening to the Holy Scriptures together, and eating and drinking together from the same bread and cup had molded them into a new community of love.

All of them started to experience support from each other in their daily struggles, many became good friends, and some even found their partners for life. Such were the remarkable fruits of spiritual community. I saw a concrete fulfillment of Jesus' promise: "When I am lifted up from the earth, I will draw all people to myself" (Jn 12:32).

LIFESIGNS

The Enigma of Emmaus

There is one sentence in the Emmaus story that leads us right into the mystery of communion. It is the sentence: "...they recognized him; but he had vanished from their sight." In the same moment that the two friends recognize him in the breaking of the bread, he is no longer there with them. When the bread is given them to eat, they no longer see him sitting with them at the table. When they eat, he has become invisible. When they enter into the most intimate communion with Jesus, the stranger—become friend—is no longer with them. Precisely when he becomes most present to them, he also becomes the absent one.

Here we touch one of the most sacred aspects of the Eucharist: the mystery that the deepest communion with

Jesus is a communion that happens in his absence....It is a communion so intimate, so holy, so sacred, and so spiritual that our corporeal senses can no longer reach it. No longer can we see him with our mortal eyes, hear him with our mortal ears, or touch him with our mortal bodies. He has come to us at that place within us where the powers of darkness and evil cannot reach, where death has no access.

WITH BURNING HEARTS

Letting Go of the Easier Friendship

When he reaches out to us and puts the bread in our hands and brings the cup to our lips, Jesus asks us to let go of the easier friendship we have had with him so far and to let go of the feelings, emotions, and even thoughts that belong to that friendship. When we eat of his body and drink of his blood, we accept the loneliness of not having him any longer at our table as a consoling partner in our conversation, helping us to deal with the losses of our daily life. It is the loneliness of the spiritual life, the loneliness of knowing that he is closer to us than we ever can be to ourselves. It's the loneliness of faith.

WITH BURNING HEARTS

Recognizing Christ and Each Other

Suddenly the two disciples, who ate the bread and recognized him, are alone again. But not with the aloneness with which they began their journey. They are alone together, and know that a new bond has been created between them. They no longer look at the ground with downcast faces. They look at each other and say: "Did our hearts not burn when he talked to us on the road and explained the scriptures to us?"

Communion creates community. Christ, living in them, brought them together in a new way. The Spirit of the risen Christ, which entered them through the eating of the bread and drinking of the cup, not only made them recognize Christ himself but also each other as members of a new community of faith. Communion makes us look at each other and speak to each other, not about the latest news, but about him who walked with us. We discover each other as people who belong together because each of us now belongs to him. We are alone, because he disappeared from our sight, but we are together because each of us is in communion with him and so have become one body through him.

WITH BURNING HEARTS

Community Leads to Mission

This new body is a spiritual body, fashioned by the Spirit of love. It manifests itself in very concrete ways: in forgiveness, reconciliation, mutual support, outreach to people in need, solidarity with all who suffer, and an ever-increasing concern for justice and peace. Thus communion not only creates community, but community always leads to mission.

WITH BURNING HEARTS

VI
COMPLETION

*To write about dying and death
without mentioning the resurrection
is like writing about sailing
without mentioning the wind.*

OUR GREATEST GIFT

*I*S LOVE STRONGER THAN DEATH?

Living Our Passages Well

*D*eath is a passage to new life. That sounds very beautiful, but few of us desire to make this passage. It might be helpful to realize that our final passage is preceded by many earlier passages. When we are born we make a passage from life in the womb to life in the family. When we go to school we make a passage from life in the family to life in the larger community When we get married we make a passage from a life with many options to a life committed to one person. When we retire we make a passage from a life of clearly defined work to a life asking for new creativity and wisdom.

Each of these passages is a death leading to new life. When we live these passages well, we are becoming more prepared for our final passage.

Bread for the Journey

Traveling With the Eyes of God

*T*raveling—seeing new sights, hearing new music, and meeting new people—is...exhilarating. But when we have no home to return to where someone will ask us, "How was your trip?" we might be less eager to go. Traveling is joyful when we travel with the eyes and ears of those who love us, who want to see our slides and hear our stories. This is what life is about. It is being sent on a trip by a loving God, who is waiting at home for our return and is eager to watch the slides we took and hear about the friends we made. When we travel with the eyes and ears of the God who sent us, we will see wonderful sights, hear wonderful sounds, meet wonderful people . . . and be happy to return home.

BREAD FOR THE JOURNEY

"Do You Love Me?"

*W*hen I was a small child I kept asking my father and mother: "Do you love me?" I asked that question so often and so persistently that it became a source of irritation to my parents. Even though they assured me hundreds of times that they loved me I never seemed fully satisfied with their answers and kept on asking the same question. Now, many years later, I realize that I wanted a response they couldn't give. I wanted them to love me with an everlasting love. I know that this was the case because my question "Do you love me?" was always accompanied by the question "Do I have to die?" Somehow, I must have known that if my parents would love me with a total, unlimited, unconditional love, I would never die.

HERE AND NOW

The Autumn of Life

The autumn leaves can dazzle us with their magnificent colors: deep red, purple, yellow, gold, bronze, in countless variations and combinations. Then, shortly after having shown their unspeakable beauty, they fall to the ground and die. The barren trees remind us that winter is near. Likewise, the autumn of life has the potential to be very colorful: wisdom, humor, care, patience, and joy may bloom splendidly just before we die. As we look at the barren trees and remember those who have died, let us be grateful for the beauty we saw in them and wait hopefully for a new spring.

Dying is a gradual diminishing and final vanishing over the horizon of life. When we watch a sailboat leaving port and moving toward the horizon, it becomes smaller and smaller until we can no longer see it. But we must trust that someone is standing on a faraway shore seeing that same sailboat become larger and larger until it reaches its new harbor. Death is a painful loss. When we return to our homes after a burial, our hearts are in grief. But when we think about the One standing at the other shore eagerly waiting to welcome our beloved friend into a new home, a smile can break through our tears.

BREAD FOR THE JOURNEY

The Resurrection:
A Hidden Event

The resurrection of Jesus is a hidden event. Jesus didn't rise from the dead to prove to those who had crucified him that they had made a mistake or to confound his opponents. Nor did he rise to impress the rulers of his time or to force anyone to believe. Jesus' resurrection was the full affirmation of his Father's love. He showed himself only to those who knew about this love. He made himself known as the risen Lord only to a handful of his close friends. Probably no other event in human history has had such importance while at the same time remaining so unspectacular. The world didn't notice Jesus' resurrection; only a few knew, those to whom Jesus had chosen to show himself and whom he wanted to send out to annouce God's love to the world.

The hiddenness of Jesus' resurrection is important to me. Although the resurrection of Jesus is the cornerstone of my faith, it is not something to use as an argument, nor is it something to use to reassure people. It somehow doesn't take death seriously enough to say to a dying person, "Don't be afraid. After your death you will be resurrected as Jesus was, meet all your friends again, and be forever happy in the presence of God." This suggests that after death everything will be basically the same, except that our troubles will be gone. Nor does it take seriously Jesus himself, who did not live through his own death as if it were little else than a necessary passage to a better life. Finally, it doesn't take seriously the dying,

who, like us, know nothing about what is beyond this
time- and place-bound existence.

OUR GREATEST GIFT

Expression of God's Faithfulness

The resurrection does not solve our problems about
dying and death. It is not the happy ending to our life's
struggle, nor is it the big surprise that God has kept in store
for us. No, the resurrection is the expression of God's
faithfulness to Jesus and to all God's children. Through the
resurrection, God has said to Jesus, "You are indeed my
beloved Son, and my love is everlasting," and to us God has
said, "You indeed are my beloved children, and my love is
everlasting." The resurrection is God's way of revealing to us
that nothing that belongs to God will ever go to waste.

The resurrection doesn't answer any of our curious
questions about life after death, such as How will it be?
How will it look? But it does reveal to us that, indeed,
love is stronger than death. After that revelation, we
must remain silent, leave the whys, wheres, hows, and
whens behind, and simply trust.

OUR GREATEST GIFT

A Story

Recently, a friend told me a story about twins talking
to each other in the womb. The sister said to the brother,
"I believe there is life after birth." Her brother protested
vehemently, "No, no, this is all there is. This is a dark and

cozy place, and we have nothing else to do but to cling to the cord that feeds us." The little girl insisted, "There must be something more than this dark place. There must be something else, a place with light where there is freedom to move." Still she could not convince her twin brother.

After some silence, the sister said hesitantly, "I have something else to say, and I'm afraid you won't believe that, either, but I think there is a mother." Her brother became furious. "A mother!" he shouted. "What are you talking about? I have never seen a mother, and neither have you. Who put that idea in your head? As I told you, this place is all we have. Why do you always want more? This is not such a bad place, after all. We have all we need, so let's be content."

The sister was quite overwhelmed by her brother's response and for a while didn't dare say anything more. But she couldn't let go of her thoughts, and since she had only her twin brother to speak to, she finally said, "Don't you feel these squeezes every once in a while? They're quite un-pleasant and sometimes even painful." "Yes," he answered. "What's special about that?" "Well," the sister said, "I think that these squeezes are there to get us ready for another place, much more beautiful than this, where we will see our mother face-to-face. Don't you think that's exciting?"

The brother didn't answer. He was fed up with the foolish talk of his sister and felt that the best thing would be simply to ignore her and hope that she would leave him alone.

This story may help us to think about death in a new way. We can live as if this life were all we had, as if death were absurd and we had better not talk about it; or we can choose to claim our divine childhood and trust that death is the painful but blessed passage that will bring us face-to-face with our God.

OUR GREATEST GIFT

Waiting to Be Lifted Up With Christ

Waiting for Christ's second coming and waiting for the resurrection are one and the same. The second coming is the coming of the risen Christ, raising our mortal bodies with him in the glory of God. Jesus' resurrection and ours are central to our faith. Our resurrection is as intimately related to the resurrection of Jesus as our belovedness is related to the belovedness of Jesus. Paul is very adamant on this point. He says, "If there is no resurrection of the dead, then Christ cannot have been raised either, and if Christ has not been raised, then our preaching is without substance, and so is your faith" (1 Cor 15:13–14).

Indeed, our waiting is for the risen Christ to lift us up with him in his eternal life with God. It is from the perspective of Jesus' resurrection and our own that his life and ours derive their full significance. "If our hope in Christ has been for this life only," Paul says, "we are of all people the most pitiable" (1 Cor 15:18). We don't need to be pitied, because as followers of Jesus we can look far beyond the limits of our short lives on earth and trust that nothing we are living now in the body will go to waste.

BREAD FOR THE JOURNEY

$\mathcal{E}$PILOGUE

A friend once gave me a beautiful
photograph of a water lily.
I asked him how he had been able
to take such a splendid picture.
With a smile he said,
"Well, I had to be very patient and very attentive.
It was only after a few hours of compliments
that the lily was willing to let me take her picture."

CLOWNING IN ROME

THE LION IN
THE MARBLE

The Secret

There once was a sculptor working hard with his hammer and chisel on a large block of marble. A little boy who was watching him saw nothing more than large and small pieces of stone falling away left and right. He had no idea what was happening. But when the boy returned to the studio a few weeks later, he saw to his great surprise, a large, powerful lion sitting in the place where the marble had stood. With great excitement the boy ran to the sculptor and said, "Sir, tell me, how did you know there was a lion in the marble?"

The little boy's question to the sculptor is a very real question, perhaps the most important question of all. The answer is, "I knew there was a lion in the marble because before I saw the lion in the marble I saw him in my own heart. The secret is that it was the lion in my heart who recognized the lion in the marble."

The practice of contemplative prayer is the discipline by which we begin to see God in our heart. It is a careful attentiveness to God who dwells in the center of our being such that through the recognition of God's presence we allow God to take possession of all our senses. Through the discipline of prayer we awaken ourselves to the God in us and let God enter into our heartbeat and our breathing, into our thoughts and emotions, our hearing, seeing, touching, and tasting.

CLOWNING IN ROME

Knowing God by Heart

It is by being awake to this God in us that we can see God in the world around us. The great mystery of the contemplative life is not that we see God in the world, but that God within us recognizes God in the world. God speaks to God, Spirit speaks to Spirit, heart speaks to heart. Contemplation, therefore, is a participation in this divine self recognition. It is the divine Spirit praying in us who makes our world transparent and opens our eyes to the presence of the divine Spirit in all that surrounds us. It is with our heart of hearts that we see the heart of the world....

To know God in the world requires knowing God by heart.

CLOWNING IN ROME

The Created Order As Sacrament

When God took on flesh in Jesus Christ, the uncreated and the created, the eternal and the temporal, the divine and the human, became united. This unity meant that all that is mortal now points to the immortal, all that is finite now points to the infinite....

BREAD FOR THE JOURNEY

A New Mysticism

Looking at the magnificent photographs of planet Earth taken from outer space, and reading the comments of the astronauts and cosmonauts, I had a sense of being introduced to a new mysticism. The observations made from outer space seem very similar to those made from inner space. They both reveal the precariousness of life, the unity of the human family, the responsibility of the "seer," the power of love, and the mystery of God. James Irwin, who flew on *Apollo 15* in July 1971, writes:

> The Earth reminded us of a Christmas tree ornament hanging in the blackness of space. As we got farther and farther away it diminished in size. Finally it shrank to the size of a marble, the most beautiful marble you can imagine. That beautiful, warm, living object looked so fragile, so delicate, that if you touched it with a finger it would crumble and fall apart. Seeing this has to change a man, has to make a man appreciate the creation of God and the love of God.

THE HOME PLANET, EDITED BY KEVIN W. KELLEY, ADDISON-WESLEY PUBLISHING CO., 1988)

All the astronauts and cosmonauts were overwhelmed by the unspeakable beauty of their own home, the planet Earth, and in some way or another raised the question

"How can we care better for our own home?" Seeing your home planet as a precious little gem that needs care and protection is a deeply mystical experience that can only be captured by words such as *grace* and *responsibility*.... The astronauts and cosmonauts gave words to my own experience of priesthood. It is a grace, it allows me to see a vision, and it is a call to let others know what I have seen; it is a long loneliness and an inexpressible joy.

SABBATICAL JOURNEY

The Holiness of Planet Earth

In recent decades we have become particularly aware of the crucial importance of our relationship with nature. As long as we relate to the trees, the rivers, the mountains, the fields, and the oceans as properties we can manipulate according to our real or fabricated needs, nature remains opaque and does not reveal to us its true being. When a tree is nothing but a potential chair, it ceases to tell us much about growth; when a river is only a dumping place for industrial wastes, it can no longer speak to us about movement; and when a flower is nothing more than a model for a plastic decoration, it has little to say about the simple beauty of life.

When we relate to nature primarily as a property to be used, it becomes opaque—an opaqueness that in our society manifests itself as pollution. The dirty rivers, the smog-filled skies, the strip-mined hills, and the ravaged woods are sad signs of our false relationship with nature.

Our difficult and very urgent task is to realize that nature is not primarily a property to be possessed, but a gift to be received with admiration and gratitude. Only when we make a deep bow to the rivers, oceans, hills, and mountains that offer us a home, only then can they become transparent and reveal to us their real meaning.

CLOWNING IN ROME

Making the Vision Come True

The marvelous vision of the peaceable Kingdom, in which all violence has been overcome and all men, women, and children live in loving unity with nature, calls for its realization in our day-to-day lives. Instead of being an escapist dream, it challenges us to anticipate what it promises. Every time we forgive our neighbor, every time we make a child smile, every time we show compassion to a suffering person, every time we arrange a bouquet of flowers, offer care to tame or wild animals, prevent pollution, create beauty in our homes and gardens, and work for peace and justice among peoples and nations we are making the vision come true.

We must remind one another constantly of the vision. Whenever it comes alive in us we will find new energy to live it out, right where we are. Instead of making us escape real life, this beautiful vision gets us involved.

BREAD FOR THE JOURNEY

Being Sent Into the World

*E*ach of us has a mission in life. Jesus prays to his Father for his followers, saying, "As you sent me into the world, I have sent them into the world" (Jn 17:18).

We seldom realize fully that we are sent to fulfill God-given tasks. We act as if *we* have to choose how, where, and with whom to live. We act as if we were simply dropped down in creation and have to decide how to entertain ourselves until we die. But we were sent into the world by God, just as Jesus was. Once we start living our lives with that conviction, we will soon know what we were sent to do.

BREAD FOR THE JOURNEY

Fulfilling a Mission

*W*hen we live our lives as missions, we become aware that there is a home from which we are sent and to which we have to return. We start thinking about ourselves as people who are in a faraway country to bring a message or work on a project, but only for a certain amount of time. When the message has been delivered and the project is finished, we want to return home to give an account of our mission and to rest from our labors.

BREAD FOR THE JOURNEY

A Writer's Evening Prayer

Tonight, O Lord, I heard you speak to the Samaritan woman. You said: "Anyone who drinks the water that I shall give will never be thirsty again; the water that I shall give will turn into a spring inside him, welling up to eternal life." What words! They are worth many hours, days, and weeks of reflection.…The water that you give turns into a spring. Therefore, I do not have to be stingy with your gift, O Lord. I can freely let the water come from my center and let anyone who desires drink from it. Perhaps I will even see this spring in myself when others come to it to quench their thirst. So often, Lord, I doubt that there is a spring in me; so often I am afraid that it has dried up or has been filled with sand. But others keep believing in the spring in me even when I do not.

Let the spring of this year and the spring of water in me give me joy, O Lord, my hope and my Redeemer. Amen.

A CRY FOR MERCY

AFTERWORD

To you who have read some or all of these meditations I want to say: Do not stop here. Continue on your own. My words were only to encourage you to find your own words, and my thoughts were only to help you discover your own thoughts. What I have written in this book is an expression of my own personal spiritual journey, bound by my own personality, time, place, and circumstances. Your spiritual journey is as unique as mine; it has its own unique beauty and unique boundaries.

My hope is that the description of God's love in *my* life will give you the freedom and the courage to discover—and maybe also describe—God's love in *yours*.

HERE AND NOW

SELECTED
BIBLIOGRAPHY
BOOKS BY HENRI NOUWEN

Intimacy: Essays in Pastoral Psychology. HarperSanFrancisco, 1969.

Creative Ministry. New York: Doubleday Image Books, 1971.

With Open Hands. Notre Dame: Ave Maria Press, 1972, revised edition, 1995.

Thomas Merton, Contemplative Critic. 1972. New revised edition: Liguori, Mo.: Liguori/Triumph, 1981.

The Wounded Healer: Ministry in Contemporary Society. New York: Doubleday Image Books, 1972.

Aging: The Fulfillment of Life. Doubleday Image Books, 1974.

Out of Solitude: Three Meditations on the Christian Life. Notre Dame: Ave Maria Press, 1974.

Reaching Out: The Three Movements of the Spiritual Life. New York, Doubleday, 1975.

Genesee Diary: Report From a Trappist Monastery. New York: Doubleday, 1976.

The Living Reminder: Service and Prayer in Memory of Jesus Christ. 1971. New revised edition: HarperSanFrancisco, 1981.

Clowning in Rome: Reflections on Solitude, Celibacy, Prayer and Contemplation. 1979. New revised edition: New York, Doubleday, 2001.

In Memoriam. Notre Dame: Ave Maria Press, 1980.

The Way of the Heart: Desert Spirituality and Contemporary Ministry. New York: Ballantine Books, 1981.

Making All Things New: An Invitation to the Spiritual Life. Harper SanFrancisco, 1981.

A Cry for Mercy: Prayers From the Genesee. Maryknoll, N.Y.: Orbis Books, 1981.

Compassion: A Reflection on the Christian Life, co-authored with Don McNeill and Douglas Morrison. New York: Doubleday Image Books, 1982.

A Letter of Consolation. HarperSanFrancisco, 1982.

Gracias! A Latin American Journal. HarperSanFrancisco, 1983.

Love in a Fearful Land: A Guatemalan Story. Notre Dame: Ave Maria Press, 1985.

Lifesigns: Intimacy, Fecundity and Ecstasy in Christian Perspective. New York: Doubleday Image Books, 1986.

Behold the Beauty of the Lord: Praying With Icons. Notre Dame: Ave Maria Press, 1987.

Letters to Marc About Jesus. HarperSanFrancisco, 1988.

The Road to Daybreak: A Spiritual Journey. Doubleday Image Books, 1988.

In the Name of Jesus: Reflections on Christian Leadership. New York: Crossroad, 1989.

Heart Speaks to Heart. Notre Dame: Ave Maria Press, 1989.

Beyond the Mirror: Reflections on Death and Life. Crossroad, 1990.

Walk With Jesus: Stations of the Cross. Maryknoll, N.Y.: Orbis Books, 1990.

The Return of the Prodigal Son: A Story of Homecoming. New York: Doubleday, 1992.

Life of the Beloved: Spiritual Living in a Secular World. New York, Crossroad, 1992.

Jesus and Mary: Finding Our Sacred Center. Cincinnati: St. Anthony Messenger Press, 1993.

Here and Now: Living in the Spirit. New York: Crossroad, 1994.

Our Greatest Gift: A Meditation on Dying and Caring. HarperSanFrancisco, 1994.

With Burning Hearts: A Meditation on the Eucharistic Life. Maryknoll, N.Y.: Orbis Books, 1994.

Path Series: The Path of Waiting/The Path of Freedom/The Path of Power/ The Path of Peace. New York: Crossroad, 1995.

Ministry and Spirituality. Three books in one, revised, inclusive language: *Creative Ministry, The Wounded Healer*, and *Reaching Out*. New York: Continuum, 1996.

Can You Drink the Cup? Notre Dame: Ave Maria Press, 1996.

The Inner Voice of Love: A Journey Through Anguish to Freedom. New York: Doubleday, 1996.

Adam: God's Beloved. Maryknoll, N.Y.: Orbis Books, 1997.

Bread for the Journey: A Daybook of Wisdom and Faith. Harper SanFrancisco, 1997.

Spiritual Journals: Genesee Diary, Gracias! A Latin American Journal, Road to Daybreak (three books in one, revised, inclusive language). New York: Continuum, 1997.

Sabbatical Journey: The Final Year. New York: Crossroad, 1997.

Collections (Readers)

Dear, John, editor. *The Road to Peace: Writings on Peace and Justice*. Maryknoll, N.Y.: Orbis Books, 1998.

Durback, Robert, editor. *Seeds of Hope: A Henri Nouwen Reader*. New York: Bantam Books, 1989. Revised edition: Doubleday, 1997.

Garvey, John, editor. *Henri Nouwen*, The Modern Spirituality Series. Springfield: Templegate Publishers, 1988.

Greer, Wendy, editor. *The Only Necessary Thing: Living a Prayerful Life*. New York: Crossroad, 1999.

Johna, Franz, editor. *Show Me the Way: Readings for Each Day of Lent*. New York: Crossroad, 1992.

Jonas, Robert A., editor. *Henri Nouwen: Writings Selected with and Introduction by Robert A. Jonas*. Maryknoll, N.Y.: Orbis Books, 1998.

Biographical

Beumer, Juren. *Henri Nouwen: A Restless Seeking for God*. New York, Crossroad, 1997.

Ford, Michael. *Wounded Prophet: A Portrait of Henri J. M. Nouwen*. New York, Doubleday, 1999.

LaNoue, Deirdre. *The Spiritual Legacy of Henri Nouwen*. New York, Continuum, 2000.

Sources
and Permissions

The compiler wishes to express his gratitude to the following for granting permission to reproduce material of which they are the publisher or copyright holder: